BLUNDERS

Other books by Peter H. Lawrence

The Hot Line (Kingsway)

Doing What Comes Supernaturally (Kingsway)

Learning to risk mistakes for Jesus

Peter H. Lawrence
author of The Hot Line

MONARCH
Crowborough

First British edition 1994

ISBN 1 85424 248 2

British Library Cataloguing in Publication Data
A catalogue record for this book is available from the British Library.

Designed and Produced in England for
MONARCH PUBLICATIONS
Broadway House, The Broadway, Crowborough,
East Sussex TN6 1HQ by
Nuprint Ltd, Harpenden, Herts, AL5 4SE.

To my favourite daughters
Amanda, Heather and Hazel
Signs not blunders

CONTENTS

ACKNOWLEDGEMENTS

I am very grateful to everyone who allowed me to include their stories in this book, and for the helpful comments they made. I am indebted to friends from Christ Church, Burney Lane and from the Lantern Church in Merley who read my draft copy and improved the content, grammar, spelling and punctuation.

I would especially like to thank Sister Christine Morris, CA, who slaved for many hours in front of a little square screen typing the manuscript for Jesus and a pub lunch.

My praise and thanks go to God for all the signs of his grace and to my wife, Carol, and our children for their encouragement and support. I managed the blunders myself.

CHAPTER

1

Signs and Blunders

God spoke to me. As clear as a bell. While I was in the bath.[1]

I was relaxing between the sessions of a Christian conference at Brighton.[2] A group of us from the same church had made the trip together and managed to find an economical guest house near the conference centre and sea front. I was not speaking or ministering or in any way responsible for anything which was taking place. I was taking it easy, learning and enjoying myself. It was absolute heaven—until God broke in.

'Tonight I want you to walk along the sea front,' he seemed to say. 'There you'll see and recognise someone who is contemplating suicide. Engage them in conversation and give away your ticket for the meeting, where the person will be saved and restored.'

It was only a thought in the head. I couldn't really expect God to daub graffiti on the walls of a private guest house, nor did I think angels would visit me while in the bath. So I was content with just a thought. But it was clear, it was precise, and it was urgent.

I attempted to put up some nominal resistance by asking myself a few questions. Was it better for me to hear my umpteenth talk at a conference or be used in saving someone's life materially and eternally? No contest. Could I wait to test it with other Christians? No, it might be too late if correct. Was it against the teachings and commands of the Bible? Definitely not. Would it cause any great harm if I was totally wrong? Most unlikely. My opposition was minimal. I knew what I had to do.

I dressed and, without a word to anyone, left the guest house. I was greeted with soft refreshing rain, but by the time I reached the English Channel I'd come through the heavy downpour stages and had arrived at the torrential. Moisture was descending like stair-rods.

The sea front at Brighton is expansive: vast acres of roads and paths, boating ponds, paddling pools and grassy areas with formal flower arrangements. Normally it is crowded, even in April. Toddlers on tricycles, teenagers with skateboards and the elderly in wheelchairs. But this evening there was no one to be seen. I was alone. Not even mad dogs and Englishmen were out in this.

Without an umbrella I trudged up and down for an hour or so. This was a serious 'word' so with true missionary zeal I plodded on. Within a short while I felt wetter than when I'd been in the bath and after this realisation the rain didn't seem to matter any more. But there was still not another soul to be seen anywhere. As time slipped by, the hotel lights came on and I knew the meeting at the conference centre was well under way. I needed to find the person quickly before it was too late.

I prayed and prayed. 'Lord give me another "word". Show me which direction to take. Lead me to the person in need.' The response was underwhelming. No more thoughts. No feeling of power or warmth. No sense of God's presence at all.

And then at last I saw him—an Englishman with his dog, sheltering from the elements in a purpose-built hut. The Brighton Council was obviously familiar with weather such as this and had prepared for it.

Excuse me...I don't suppose...were you possibly

thinking of.... No that wouldn't do. He looked happy enough, so did the dog. I entered the haven in a more cautious and English way, trying to look nonchalantly like someone else in need of protection. 'Turned out nice,' I said, smiling like George Formby. How was he? Fine. How was the dog? Fine. How was I? Soaked. Miserable. Almost ready to jump off the pier? Not quite.

The rain eased as darkness descended and I made my way to the conference. Nobody bothered to check my badge. Terry Virgo was coming to the end of his famous Gideon sermon and the whole place was captivated.[3]

'Marvellous, wasn't it?' said a friend in the foyer afterwards, as I sought to restore myself with a cup of coffee. 'Yes, particularly good last five minutes,' I offered between sips. 'You look a little wet, Peter,' he commented. 'Yes,' I muttered, 'I feel like a little wet.'

Some will say I should have stayed out longer. Those uncomfortable with failure might think I could have been more direct with the Englishman or his dog. I have a more simple conclusion to offer—I was wrong. I made a blunder. God had not spoken to me.

That's it, I thought. Never again. What an idiot. I fall for it every time. No discernment. Any old thought which comes into my head. For ever putting my foot in it. If only I could guarantee being right. Why doesn't God turn up the volume a bit and make it easier?

'"They will all know me from the least of them to the greatest", says the Lord' (Heb 8:11). Indeed! It's just that some seem to know him better than others.

Whenever I make a mistake like this the voices of my critics ring even louder in my ears. 'Schizophrenia,' comes from the medics, 'megalomania,' from the politically orientated and 'eccentric' from my church friends. Accusations, labels, fiery darts: the post-enlightenment attack on anything claiming to be metaphysical, non-rational or supernatural. My failures are hard to bear. Each one gives ammunition to my enemies: recovery becomes difficult, perseverance daunting and growth almost impossible. Negative thoughts cannot easily be dispelled until another more positive opportunity comes along.

One Saturday morning I was doing some work in my study when I began to feel strangely warmed. I immediately stopped what I was doing, went over to an armchair, sat down, closed my eyes and waited for God to speak to me. It was almost an involuntary action. Hours of mental torment were cast aside as something indefinable stirred in my spirit. Constantly wondering how I would react next time, when it came, my reaction was comforting in its swiftness.

I prayed, 'Come Holy Spirit' and immediately my thoughts turned to Roger Jones, our lay reader and full-time Christian musician, who was ministering at another church that weekend. An interesting thought came to me: 'Tell Roger to give out this "word" at the Sunday-evening service. There will be a teenage girl present with a pain in the neck where it meets the shoulder.' And then a further instruction. 'Tell the person who sees her that the pain in the neck is not the main reason I want her to come forward.' Although it was not me who would look a fool at the church service, I didn't much fancy the idea of being wrong—again. How could I know if it was right? What test could be applied? All I seemed to have was my own inner turmoil and struggle but maybe that in itself was saying something? 'If I say, "I will not mention him or speak any more in his name," his word is in my heart like a fire, a fire shut up in my bones. I am weary of holding it in; indeed I cannot' (Jer 20:9).

I phoned my message through to Mary Jones who relayed it to her husband late on Saturday night. Roger has quite a well-known Christian music ministry both in this country and abroad. His works continue to sell well and he receives many invitations to speak in other churches of differing shades of spirituality and churchmanship. In recent years he has been faithful in giving possible 'words' from God which praying supporters have given him. During this time more people have been saved, healed and delivered than ever before and far more letters of criticism and even abuse have been sent to him. It is a costly ministry. Roger risked it and gave it out at the Sunday-evening service along with several other 'words' which he and the team received.[4]

Two teenage girls attended all the meetings. One of them was a committed Christian worshipping regularly in the church, the other a friend she had persuaded to come with her. At the very first session Roger's talk seemed to give the friend a pain in the neck. It was a genuine, physical pain which stayed with her all weekend, until after Roger's final sermon. She told her friend all about it.

When Roger gave the 'word' on Sunday evening, the Christian girl nudged her friend. 'That's for you,' she said. The friend nodded and agreed to go with her to the front. As soon as she left her chair the pain in the neck also left, never to return; but they still came forward.

Gill was waiting for them. Roger had told her the further instruction so when the girls shared their story and why they had come forward Gill asked a few sensitive questions. 'Yes' one was definitely a committed Christian but 'no' her friend was not. Encouraged by the 'word' and the physical sign in her neck, she confessed her new belief and accepted Jesus Christ as her personal Saviour. Her friend promised to look after her and nurture her in the Christian faith.

If my enthusiasm had been dampened by the Brighton rains it was certainly revived by the news Roger shared with me after the weekend. I can cope with cynical comments about coincidence, lucky guess or sheer fluke when someone is born again and enters the kingdom of God. This time the risk seemed worth while. I was ready to have another go.

One Sunday morning I was persuaded by John Leach, the Vicar of St James' Styvechale in Coventry, to preside and preach at his two morning Holy Communion services. I agreed as this would release John to be the main speaker for an East Birmingham Renewal Group weekend.[5]

It was an early start with plenty of opportunity for worry. Would the car start? How would I look in the funny 'high-church' clothes John had persuaded me to wear? Preaching in an unfamiliar church is not too difficult, but taking services these days with so many possible variations can be a nightmare. At which of the two services did John say they rang the bell three times during the communion? And... would the smartly-dressed ladies welcome the Holy Spirit at their service?

John had been at St James' for only a short while. I was worried about going there; John was terrified of me going there. I was afraid God would not come in power when I invited him to do so. John was afraid God would come in power, leaving him to pick up the pieces afterwards.

Halfway through his Sunday-morning talk at the conference, John's watch alarm went off. He immediately stopped, turned pale and asked the gathered assembly to pray. 'Peter is now asking the Holy Spirit to come on the congregation at St James',' he explained.

Eileen should not have been at St James' church that Sunday morning. She should have been in hospital, but for the second time her appointment was cancelled. She arrived carrying a 'lump of anger, resentment and depression'. Even so, the Holy Spirit came on her. As God moved gently over the congregation, I thought somebody present was suffering from bereavement—perhaps from a little while ago. Eileen's mother had died two months previously.

As I shared my thought Eileen began crying, and this is what she wrote to me afterwards: 'I realised that for the first time since she died I was truly grieving for my mother's death.... It just seemed so right that at last I could grieve properly. It felt very good and cleansing.'

Before the crying was over, the 'lump' had gone. I need not have worried. John need not have worried. God loves smartly-dressed ladies!

Being drenched on my own beside the English Channel always carried the consolation that no one I knew saw me. I did not announce my intentions to anyone beforehand. Going to a church for the first time, where a friend has invited me with fear and trembling in his heart, creates a different arena for experimentation. I was so grateful to God for the outcome. It encouraged us all to go on seeking his face, his hand and his voice.

When Jesus and his disciples moved in the power of the Holy Spirit, demons manifested, demons were discerned and demons were cast out. It was an integral part of their signs-and-wonders ministry. Many Christians today are happier with signs for salvation or healing than for deliverance, but in our experience they seem to be part of the same package.

Jenny (not her real name), from our own congregation, put the children to bed one evening despite feeling considerable discomfort. This quickly changed to severe pain and the doctor who was called out diagnosed acute appendicitis. Jenny was rushed into hospital while Christians from church began praying.

To everyone's surprise, the casualty doctor wavered in his diagnosis and admitted Jenny to a ward, put her on a drip and began monitoring her condition. This gave me the chance to visit Jenny with my wife Carol and to pray with her. During this time I said, 'I don't think the doctors will find anything wrong. I suspect this is ancestral witchcraft. Let the doctors examine you and if they let you home without an operation I'll have a go.'

It is my experience that demons do not appear on X-rays. I always prefer doctors to decide if there is anything physically wrong first and then we minister afterwards. We do, of course, pray and bind any demons which we think may be present until the medical profession have finished.

Jenny's temperature settled, the pain began to ease and the drip was removed. Five days after being admitted, she was given an ultrasound scan which revealed nothing. They were all rather perplexed but Jenny was sent home as she was now feeling a little better. We arranged a time of ministry as soon as we could.

Accompanied by Denise, I asked the Holy Spirit to come and show us the root of Jenny's problem. Demons appeared to manifest themselves strongly and noisily. Jenny saw in her mind an appalling and disturbing vision of a newly-born baby being separated from its mother and placed on an altar ready to be killed. I cannot remember too many of the details, but this is what Jenny wrote down for me:

> Peter discerned many ancestral demons connected with this incident including a 'spirit of the dagger' which we suspected had been causing the acute pains. Ancestral blood ties were broken, curses were revoked and repentance made for the sins of the ancestors. I felt demons leaving as Peter commanded them to come out. The biggest struggle was with a Jezebel spirit that seemed to be ruling over the others. After much inner pressure and struggling, followed by a bout of deep coughing, I was fairly convinced it had gone. As I write, nearly a whole year has passed since this episode and I have not had so much as a twinge of discomfort.

We received a slight hint of confirmation some time later. A close relative of Jenny was also receiving deliverance ministry when a 'word' from God was given about the child sacrifice and the Norse ancestry. History also agrees that their Norse ancestors—who can be directly traced—were involved in ritual abortions.

Verification of 'words' from God is never easy. These

days I am not completely satisfied just by words and details being correct, even if I am sure the person giving them is a Christian. I also like to be sure that the kingdom of God is advanced.

The 'word' which I received and Roger gave at the evening service may be challenged. Demons can sometimes give non-Christians a pain in the neck and take it away again. We believe there is also a Satanic network which can convey messages across some distance quite quickly. But when the person claiming the 'word' given by Christians becomes a Christian herself, then I am reasonably satisfied that the kingdom of God has been advanced. The distance involved in this particular 'word' removed the possibility of natural discernment or intelligent guesswork from first looking at the congregation. I have never been to that church.

The 'word' I gave at Styvechale is probably the easiest to doubt. To say in a church full of people that someone present has been bereaved a little while ago, is not of itself very convincing. But when that 'word' speaks to an individual, who opens herself to God's Holy Spirit and loses a lump of 'anger, resentment and depression' in the process, then I believe we have an event which sounds like God's healing.

Deliverance 'words' are notoriously difficult to justify, especially as many Christians are not yet open to this possibility. Even so, deliverance is biblical and it is related in the New Testament to the advancement of God's kingdom. Part of the 'word' for Jenny was verified by the medical profession. Further, the acute physical pain went permanently as a result of prayer for the removal of demons. There was therefore some evidence to suggest that the finger of God had been at work.

The blunder beneath the black rain-clouds of Brighton is hard to understand. I know what most Christians would like me to confess. 'You weren't right with God that week? You didn't worship, read your Bible or say your prayers? While in the bath you were having selfish, lustful or materialistic thoughts?'

My subjective opinion is that during the week at Brighton I was relaxed and happy, at peace with God, the world and everything in it. I worshipped, prayed and read my Bible every day. When the 'word' came it was silent and private. I was not trying to impress anyone.

On the other hand, the 'words' which led to salvation, healing and deliverance came at a time when I was harassed, anxious, not praying so much and struggling on with the daily round. If God gave gifts according to righteousness I would have to say the computer in heaven was playing up or someone's wires were crossed. Fortunately God doesn't give gifts according to righteousness. That is why they are called gifts not Brownie Points. Maybe the one significant factor with the three 'words' which seemed to be right was that other Christians were praying. In Brighton I was alone. In the New Testament spiritual gifts are given to the body of Christ rather than to isolated prophets as in the Old Testament.

Even so this makes it very difficult for us to teach and pass on to others. If we continually pray for each other and seek to share one another's burdens, this still does not guarantee infallibility. We long to know why. We seek more knowledge, always of course, so that we can serve God better. Or so I preach. In reality I think I want to know how and why God works at all times and in all places so that I can plan and control my own life. Anything to save me from having to trust, which I find so difficult.

More of us desire to do or see signs and wonders than to be involved in signs and blunders. No one really wants to look or be thought a fool, and wherever I go people ask me, 'How do we know when it is God? Is his bell louder than all others? How can we be sure? What if I ask him to come and he doesn't?' I always say, 'I don't know.' My experience of Brighton has been repeated many times.

There have been some sweet-sounding chimes and some awful clangers. Taken over a period of eight years I would say the joy has comfortably outweighed the pain, but I am not convinced I get more 'words' right today than before. Nor does God always come in the way in which I hope or expect him to do. Even so, God has not stopped speaking or coming.

I do not know why I experience blunders as well as signs, but this I know: whenever people are willing to be fools for Christ and seek first the kingdom of God, signs of God's grace seem to accompany them (Mk 16:17). Christianity without faith and trust may feel safer, but it is rarely as powerful, effective or rewarding.

C. Peter Wagner, the Professor of Church Growth at Fuller Theological Seminary in California, quoted these figures at a conference in 1992:

> In 1979 there were 91 million pentecostal/charismatic Christians in the world.
> In 1991 there were 410 million pentecostal/charismatic Christians in the world.[6]

If his survey is correct, then this is the greatest revival in the history of the church. We can put the Acts of the Apostles, the Jonathan Edwards, Wesley, Whitefield and all other movements of God's Spirit together and not come up with anything statistically like this. We have lived through the greatest numerical revival in the history of mankind. Why then are we not leaping about and shouting it from the rooftops in the West? Because in the same period of history, 1979-1991, the church in America remained static and the church in England declined by two per cent. We often seek after knowledge and security. Those experiencing revival seek after God.

But there are a number of problems in church life which discourage us from taking risks. Some are theological: is it not a wicked and adulterous generation which asks for a miraculous sign? If it is God who does signs why should we expect blunders as well? Can we expect everyone to be healed? Some are pastoral: if I am not healed will I be unwelcome or an embarrassment to a church with a known healing ministry? Some are practical: can we really expect signs as well as blunders in our particular congregation? Some are ecumenical: if we allow the Holy Spirit the freedom to move in our churches will it lead to greater unity? Some are political: we hear a lot about healing the sick individual but is there any hope for the nations? What is the Spirit saying to divided communities such as Ireland? And some are personal: I don't cope very well with failure and rejection. I am well liked and respected in our area. I might like to become an archdeacon or a bishop one day.

I certainly do not have all the answers but this book is written in order to share some of God's encouragements which, for me, have made the challenge of taking risks worthwhile. It has never been easy being a Christian, but I believe it has always been worth it.

Signs and Blunders is a serious title. Often we do not experience the signs of God's kingdom because we are not willing to risk making blunders ourselves. I do not fully understand the dark clouds of failure, but they do seem to follow me around and be more evident when God is about to do special things. Wheat and weeds appear to go together. Spiritual warfare is a fact of spiritual life and I believe if we want to see more signs of God's kingdom in our midst, we need to be prepared for our own blunders as well.

We begin at the cross.

Endnotes

1. A shorter version of this story first appeared in Anglican Renewal Ministries' magazine, *Anglicans for Renewal*, volume 43. It is repeated here with their kind permission.
2. 'Spiritual Warfare' conference, Brighton, 18-21 April 1988.

3. Gideon is one of three Old Testament characters whom Terry Virgo writes about in his book *Men of Destiny* (Kingsway Publications: Eastbourne, 1987).
4. Enquiries for Roger Jones to come and speak can be addressed to: Christian Music Ministries, 325 Bromford Road, Hodge Hill, Birmingham B36 8ET.
5. East Birmingham Renewal Group is a small inter-denominational fellowship of Christians working towards renewal in the church. The group prayerfully supports Roger Jones, one of its members, in his full-time, itinerant Christian work and sends out teams to teach and minister in the power of the Holy Spirit whenever churches or communities invite them to do so. They can be contacted at the CMM address above.
6. 'Challenge 2000' conference, Birmingham, February 1992.

CHAPTER

2

Meeting Jesus at the Cross

The darkly-clad figure came across the cornfield under the cloak of night. It was winter. Times were hard, but for a man of his profession a few days before Christmas was the time of times. The larders were full, the wine racks overflowed with the fruit of the vine, and the presents scattered around the foot of the trees offered rich pickings to ruthless predators.

Before him was a detached house plunged in darkness except for the obvious land-light which was shining dimly. His experienced nostrils told him that this one was empty and just right for the taking. In the fifties there were few deterrents. No automatic lights to illuminate the garden; no alarm bells to arouse the neighbours; no window-locks to present even the mildest of challenges to a skilled worker. There wasn't even a dog in this particular establishment.

As he crossed the garden swiftly and stealthily, his entry-point became obvious. The drainpipe took him easily to the balcony, the safety and security of which made opening the bedroom window an easy task for such a gifted practitioner. Nothing stirred as, silently, he entered the house.

The first room was a disappointment. Trains on the wallpaper told the story. This was the boy's bedroom. He quickly ransacked a few drawers, just in case, and was about to look further afield when the tell-tale click of a key in the front door brought the brief visit to an end. Children's voices broke the silence and the patter of small feet racing up the stairs covered the sound of a balcony door opening and a quick escape down the drainpipe to freedom in the cornfield. The thief in the night had to make do with someone else's Christmas presents this time round.

I never saw him. I was only nine at the time.

As a special treat the whole family had been swimming. When we arrived home I was desperate for the loo so I rushed through the door before the others.

I never met the burglar, but I could see that things in my room had been disturbed. Policemen came to our home, and spent longest in my bedroom. From then on I suffered bad dreams every night. They were always the same: fear of death and darkness and falling into a bottomless chasm. Being the youngest I went to bed first. Every night I kept the lights on, looked in all the cupboards and under the bed before sliding under the sheets and trying to hide from my fears. However warm it was I always insisted on the windows being closed. Even so, when the curtains were drawn in front of the balcony, I still imagined a thousand different faces behind them. The problem was not the drainpipe, balcony or curtains but the nightmares which haunted me on the inside every time I slept.

I might have coped better if the troubles had left me when dawn broke, but the new darkness was all-pervading. During the day I began avoiding all the cracks in the pavements; racing cars and lorries to lamp-posts, believing my life depended on beating them; walking round ladders and into the path of black cats. Paranoic fear, especially the fear of death, dominated my nights and days.

This was one more pain to add to the many others which dominated my childhood. Ironically, they prepared a path for me which led to the cross. As with so many other conversions, the Holy Spirit used the circumstances of my life, together with my background and upbringing, to open my eyes to a problem. When I knew that I needed a saviour I was ready to hear and receive Jesus.

My paternal grandfather died in 1924. He was a professional soldier who survived the First World War because he remained in England to train the raw recruits. He died of pneumonia and was buried with full military honours. My father was only a little boy when it happened, but the consequences were far reaching. He and his younger brother faced hardship in the twenties and thirties, being brought up by a widow who needed to take in washing in order to survive. My dad was determined his family would never suffer as he did.

Frequently, when I was very young, he would leave home before I was awake and return after I'd fallen asleep. He worked on Saturdays, went to church on Sunday mornings and spent the rest of the time recovering. With the exception of holiday times, my sister and I developed a relationship with our father in occasional five-minute snippets, often when he was far from relaxed. By the time I was eleven we had moved home five times as his drive to succeed brought one promotion after another. I was driven to succeed as well.

My dad did not have the role of a father modelled to him. Poverty was miserable; success took him away from misery. Love was therefore seen as helping me to succeed. Passing the eleven-plus examination and attending grammar school were everything. Against the odds my father passed his test and went on to become a pharmaceutical chemist and a captain in the army during the war. He began in a terraced house in Yorkshire and ended his life in a detached house in Virginia Water, Surrey. I simply had to pass the eleven plus. I received lectures about it every week and was given private lessons from the age of eight, which required constant homework. Anxiety and pressure were with me from an early age. The nightmares and fears which the burglar brought merely added to my problems.

The day I took my eleven plus in York I was nervous, panicky and, in the end, very angry. There were 120 questions to answer on one paper and for months in my private lessons and rehearsals I'd always done them in the time allowed. This time I did only 90. I couldn't do a particular question and instead of moving on to the others I stubbornly disobeyed all my training as I allowed anger to rise inside me. Voices within were saying, 'Serve him right.' Despite this aberration, I still passed and went to the grammar school in Surrey, following our move to my fifth home. Sometimes, as I look back, I wonder if my teenage years would have been less pressured and more enjoyable had I failed.

I was extremely unhappy and became somewhat rebellious. Performance orientation has an ever-receding horizon. After the eleven plus it was being in the 'A' stream. When I dropped into the 'B' stream and came bottom of the class, it was not being put in the 'C' stream. End-of-term examinations and school reports continually hung over me like the Sword of Damocles. I thought I would only be any good, acceptable, if I went to university.

Throughout my time at secondary school, I had no real friends and was often teased about my size and shape—I can still get into my under-thirteen football shirt. Fortunately I was good at sport, enjoyed it and did well.

When I was fourteen we took the usual end-of-term examinations in December. I sat at the back of the class between two rogues who regularly cheated by balancing books on their knees throughout each exam. They were never caught, bragging about it each time and daring me to do it with them during the Religious Knowledge test.

Now if there was one subject in which I did not need to cheat it was RK. Having attended church and Sunday school every week of my life, I had an enormous advantage over the majority of boys in my class, but the challenge to be one of them was on. Would I dare? I would do anything to be accepted.

During the examination the master walked to the back of the classroom and as he did so the books on my friends' laps disappeared. With the skill which comes from much practice, they slid their books forward and held them firmly against the recess under the desk with their knees. I was not so skilful or well practised and was caught red-faced and knock-kneed as my book crashed to the floor.

The teacher wrote it on my school-report book and the headmaster struck me several times with the book when he interviewed me. I couldn't face my father seeing it so I altered it skilfully and successfully on the way home.

In January the report book was returned and nothing was said. I now had guilt and fear of being found out to add to nightmares, fear of death, fear of failure and lack of friends. Unlike my time at junior school, my work was now always poor. I was frequently late home due to being put in detention which in turn led to more friction and cross words at home. And—whenever I went out with anyone—it was not easy avoiding the cracks in the pavement without being noticed.

Towards the end of the summer term, lessons were cancelled for sports' day. Sport was the other big drive in my father's life—and mine. I was selected by my house for the triple jump. The headmaster, governors and honoured guests sat in a line along the runway and sand-pit and as I walked nervously past them on my way to the first jump, the headmaster beckoned me to him.

'Lawrence,' he said sternly, 'I want to see you in my study first thing in the morning.'

Such beautiful timing. I thought I knew why. No reports were written at Easter, only at Christmas and at the end of the summer term. This was the first time my report book would have been read since its return in January. I did not jump very well. The next day my worst fears were realised. I was informed in the morning that the headmaster would be writing to my father about the cheating episode and my subsequent alteration of the school report.

The headmaster was one of the church wardens at our local church and my father was the other. There was no escape. The letter didn't arrive the next day, nor the next, nor the one after that. Life was not good. More than ever before, anger, fear, resentment and guilt tormented me in the daylight and increased the size of my monsters by night. Eventually it came. There were words, and tears, and the term was over.

During the following summer holidays I went to Jersey on a CPAS Pathfinder camp with a group from my own church.[1] Our youth leaders had spent some time trying to persuade me to go and I was now pleased to be leaving school and family behind for a while.

The Romans and Normans had arrived before me and left their mark. Beside the port of Gorey stands Mount Orgueil Castle from which approaching French visitors can easily be spotted. It was near here that I became a Christian.

Despite the beauty of Jersey I still had my problems. They came with me as they lived inside me. We stayed in Gorey, sleeping in dormitories where much teasing and jocularity took place. I managed to hold my own and keep in with the crowd but it was never easy.

I needed forgiveness; I needed a friend; I needed someone to take away my fear of darkness and death. Above all else I needed someone to accept me just as I was without my having to earn their favour.

On one occasion, the challenge was on to climb the rock-face from the beach and enter the castle without paying. It was a hard struggle, especially for someone with a fear of heights, but fortunately we all failed. Walking along the seashore we encountered many other castles with flags on them and small children being photographed beside their achievements. Random thoughts went through my mind. Castles on the ground and in the air; people of all ages trying to climb very high; ambition, success, flag on the top; king of the castle. At fourteen I was already tired of the world: people spending money they didn't have, to buy things they didn't need, to impress people they didn't like. I made the decision that I no longer wanted to impress anyone.

In our meetings they told us about a man who turned the world upside down and I listened intently. I'd heard about him before of course, but never with such pain and need in my heart.

Jesus never built any castles, wrote any books or travelled beyond his small native land. Instead of climbing very high he came down and knelt very low. Though he was rich yet for our sakes he became poor (2 Cor 8:9). King of kings and Lord of lords (Rev 19:6), he came down from heaven and was born in a stable (Lk 2:7). Even though all things were made through him and there was nothing made that has been made without him (Jn 1:1), he submitted himself to Joseph and Mary (Lk 2:51), came under the Jewish authorities and regularly attended the synagogue (Lk 4:16).

After vandals damaged his home in Capernaum (Mk 2:1–4) and crowds made it impossible for him to stay there, Jesus became like a tramp with nowhere to lay his head (Mt 8:20). He needed to catch fish to pay his taxes (Mt 17:27). At all times Jesus only did what the Father told him to do (Jn 5:19), including the menial servant's task of washing the disciples' feet (Jn 13:5). Eventually he became obedient to death, even death on a cross (Phil 2:8).

Our leaders majored on the cross. The real king of the castle had become for us the dirty rascal. Despised and rejected, Jesus, the King of the Jews, bore our own sin in his body on the tree (1 Pet 2:24).

One of the speakers wrote a song about the cross especially for our camp. I particularly remember the verses about the penitent thief who went with Jesus to paradise when Good Friday was finished. Over thirty years later I can still recall the line, 'He had nothing he could offer.' That was me: a failure; bottom of the class; overweight and teased; embarrassed in a dormitory of teenage lads about my daytime superstitions and night-time fears. Jesus loved and accepted the thief, but would he love and accept me?

Our teachers shared with us the way to receive his love and acceptance: The cross is the place where Jesus always calls us to meet him. For now we are not asked to be lifted high and meet him in the air, but to stoop low and descend the stairway of humility. To meet Jesus in this life, the path is always downwards.

I thought about Jesus' invitation as the steps we needed to take before we could meet him at the cross were explained to us. We begin by admitting our own failures. It is hard to be told that our best efforts are not good enough, but Isaiah goes even further. 'All our righteous acts are like filthy rags,' he declares (Is 64:6). The road to the cross is littered with good deeds which people have cast off and laid aside. They will never take us to Jesus. Abandoning our own attempts to make ourselves acceptable becomes the first step down towards the cross. Rather than presenting a difficulty or even a challenge, this came to me as something of a relief. No more trying to achieve love and acceptance by my own efforts: by God's grace alone am I saved.

As we come down the narrow way which leads to

Jesus, we see others whose known sins appear much worse than our own. In comparison our lives don't seem so bad. Paul writes, 'The wages of sin is death' (Rom 6:23). It is offensive to good-living people to be told our little sins deserve the same punishment as our neighbours' whoppers, but it is an offence which must be swallowed with our pride if we are to proceed further.

I needed to pause here. The rogues who sat either side of me in the Religious Knowledge test often stole from shops as well as cheated in exams. They had escaped scot free and received good school reports. But that was their problem and I wanted to be right before God. I chose to forgive.

Jesus said, 'You still lack one thing. Sell everything you have and give to the poor' (Lk 18:22). It is not possible to serve God and mammon. The eye of a needle is too narrow for a rich man and his camels to pass through. The possessions need to be left behind. He who builds up treasure on earth in large city dwellings will not easily find his way to Calvary. It is outside the city wall.

In my short life, to the envy of some of my colleagues, I did not lack any material thing, but this never brought peace. I wanted to leave the lust for worldly goods behind. As a non wage-earner, the material thing in my life which could keep me from God was giving too high a priority to sport. This needed to be considered very carefully. It is even harder for youngsters today as much amateur sport is played on Sunday mornings.

Possessions are one thing; families are another. Most of us would be willing to give up everything we own, if it was necessary, for the sake of our loved ones, but to give up our loved ones.... Jesus said, 'Anyone who loves his father or mother more than me is not worthy of me; anyone who loves his son or daughter more than me is not worthy of me' (Mt 10:37). Just as God gave his only son for us, so he asks us to put him before even our nearest and dearest.

The mention of family made me feel distinctly uncomfortable. It was not so much the putting of Jesus before family—this is relatively easy for most teenagers in nominally Christian countries—it was the thought that if I became a Christian I would have to tell them. Unwittingly I had anticipated the final step.

The person who met Jesus at the cross on Good Friday was on a cross himself (Lk 23:42–43). If we are to come that close to Jesus ourselves we are called to share in his sufferings. Jesus said, 'If anyone would come after me, he must deny himself and take up his cross and follow me. For whoever wants to save his life will lose it, but whoever loses his life for me and for the gospel will save it' (Mk 8:34–35).

This was undoubtedly the hard one for me. Those who accepted Christ at the camp were encouraged to share it publicly at the meeting and to tell their families and friends at home. 'If you confess with your mouth, "Jesus is Lord," and believe in your heart that God raised him from the dead, you will be saved' (Rom 10:9).

I had only cheated in the first place to win friends and influence people, but now I was being challenged to alienate the jeerers even more. Despite the Christian nature of the camp, few of the others in my dormitory seemed to be believers and I couldn't face further rejection. I wondered if Jesus might understand and be sympathetic. I thought I might try him for myself and see if anything happened. Then perhaps—who knows—I might just tell one or two.

We were invited to meet with a leader if we wanted to ask Jesus into our lives, but I was never very comfortable with teachers so I went straight to the top, privately. Late at night, as the lights and torches finally went out and the noise in the dormitory subsided, I recalled all I'd heard in my mind and made a decision. I invited Jesus Christ to be the Lord and Saviour of my life and then went to sleep.

When the rising bell was sounded in the morning, I

awoke to the most dramatic of dawns. There was a glow on my face and a peace in my heart. For the first time in five years I had slept through without nightmares. I dressed quickly, ran outside, and was grateful no one saw me as I rushed to the nearest pavement and deliberately jumped on all the cracks. I was free! The world was different: brighter, fresher, cleaner. It seemed to smell and taste better than I could ever remember. When I came in for breakfast I couldn't understand why the others weren't all as excited as I was about this brand-new day.

I attended all the voluntary Bible studies, let rip in the worship to the embarrassment of all around and told one or two well-chosen people what had occurred. Somehow they seemed to know already.

I remember watching the news on the television. It was the same then as it is now. Death, death and more death: car crashes, plane crashes, murder, disasters and war. Death, not life, makes news. As I took in the day's particular tragedies, two things struck me.

First, I was not afraid of death any more. I was now happy to go to bed, alone, in the dark. Later, still as a teenager, I learnt to play the organ and would often lock up the church late at night, plunge the building into complete darkness and walk home on my own through the graveyard without thinking twice about it. Instantly, what had been a great weakness in my life became a strength.

Secondly, I realised how the gift of eternal life made the world's lust to achieve, possess and dominate appear so futile. The steps which can take us up to plant our flags on the top of our own castles also have a down side. Once we have our own house, car, good job and two-point-four children, the only way is down. The day surely comes when our children leave school, fly the nest and get married. There is an ocean of emptiness in our castle.

We begin to forget things. The cricket trousers seem to shrink in the cupboard during the winter. The younger members of the team appear to be doing better than us. We retire from work. For some it is the first death. Smaller home, smaller car, less money. Kicking our heels at home with very little sense of worth and fulfilment. But worse is to come. Our partner dies. People are very good but soon they forget. Alone with reminiscences. Alone with letters and photo albums and the presentation clock. Simply alone.

Eventually we cannot cope. The old people's home beckons. Sight fades and hearing dulls. For some, the end of life may be just like the beginning. We cannot stand, walk or feed ourselves. We have to wear nappies and others have to change them for us. One day our name appears in the obituary column with many others. The family gather at the solicitors. 'How much did he leave?' they ask. The legalist looks at them with a straight face and replies in a matter-of-fact manner. 'All of it. He took none of it with him.'

We bring nothing into the world and we take nothing out.

This is the futility of the world's rostrum. All is vanity. It is here today and gone tomorrow. Satan's path always has its pay-day.

For me, however, as one who had just received so much, the present blessings in contrast to the way of the world were something very special. I received all I needed.

a) The guilt of the past, and especially the last nine months since the December exams, was washed away in a moment. I knew I had sinned and regretted it deeply, but now I felt as though it had never happened. I was forgiven.

b) Receiving Christ did not initially help me to make friends—discovering the joys of the body of Christ was still some way in the distance—but now I had one special friend. I could go into my own room, even when it was dark, and pray, read the Bible and enjoy the thrill of

Christian books testifying to the presence and power of Christ today. I was not mature. I was not a great witness to my family or those at school, but I did enjoy being with my friend, alone in my room.

c) To go to bed in peace and wake in joy after five years of unremitting nightmares was virtually indescribable, and it happened again and again.

d) The struggle to achieve acceptance and love was now over. This was undoubtedly the greatest joy. Like Paul, Augustine and Martin Luther, the peace came when I gave up trying and started trusting. It was OK to be, I no longer needed to become. Meeting Jesus at the cross only seems like sacrifice in the eyes of the world. To the believer all else is rubbish compared to the surpassing greatness of knowing Christ Jesus as Lord (Phil 3:8).

I came home full of evangelical zeal and told my friends and family all about it. My parents said it would wear off in a week or two and not to worry about it. I am pleased to say God has kept me so far for thirty-two years and I'm still as excited by him now as I was then. I shall be forever grateful to Egham parish church and its youth leaders who took me to Jersey; the speakers who shared their faith with us, and Jesus, the Good Shepherd, who found me and saved me. To him be all the glory.

Whenever we meet Jesus at the cross the only way is up. Having been buried with Christ beneath the waters of death, we now rise with him to new life. Having already died, death no longer has dominion over us. Whoever believes in Jesus will never die (Jn 11). Even the elderly geriatric with memories of past glories can say that in Christ the best is yet to be. 'He is no fool who gives what he cannot keep to gain what he cannot lose.'[2]

There are many reasons why people will not risk making blunders for the sake of the King and the kingdom, but the person who has already died has less of a problem. He has nothing more to lose. He may not become an archdeacon or a bishop, but those who have met the King of Kings and been adopted into his family aren't usually too bothered, one way or the other. Everyone who meets Jesus at the cross and dies with Christ is ready for signs and blunders.

We will look at the signs first.

Endnotes

1. I am delighted to say the Church Pastoral Aid Society's camps for young people are still in operation and I would highly recommend them.
2. I first heard this saying attributed to Jim Elliot, the Ecuador martyr, but I am not sure if he was the first to use it.

CHAPTER

3

Signs of the Kingdom

Egham parish church in Surrey has become a more prominent feature in the town since the by-pass was built across the corner of its graveyard. Those who live near it will tell you how the bells are very Anglican and very tuneful, expertly played and clearly heard even on practice nights. The building itself is not so obviously Church of England, being built in the shape of a rectangle rather than a cross. There is virtually no chancel area, giving the impression more of a Methodist church with the choir leading worship from the upstairs gallery at the back.

Being the nearest parish church to Runnymede, where the English Barons encouraged King John to sign the Magna Carta, it is a place of considerable historical interest. Replicas of the barons' shields hang from the gallery on the inside of the building while outside all kinds of interesting tombs surround the present-day worshipping saints. The last official duel in England was fought nearby and the loser was buried in the churchyard.

When my father was church warden he had access to some of the ancient documents. Recorded in one of the old registers was the story of the verger who apparently made a mistake in the parish records and immediately went out and hanged himself. Achievement and success seem to have been taken seriously in bygone days as well!

In 1744 John Wesley preached at Egham church. He was not invited to speak inside but when the service was over he stood outside, took the same text as the preacher and told the assembled crowd what ought to have been said.

This is the church which nurtured me in the Christian faith. I was taught well and learnt to love the Bible and value the daily quiet time alone with God. The preaching was always first class and occasional missions like the one led by Dick Rees still remain in my memory as high points in my early Christian days.

A few years after I was saved in Jersey, I attended morning prayer in my home church. I stood to sing the traditional hymn 'My God how wonderful thou art', and as I did so I began to forget about myself and think of Jesus. I sensed power come over me. I wanted to cry. It felt as though someone was pouring a bucket of love all over me. I wished I could have died at that moment, so great was my desire to be in heaven. In some ways I felt I was already there. I knew from then on that Christianity was not just a matter of words or pie in the sky when you die, but something very real and wonderful which was available here and now.

Until that point my Christianity had always been a rather selfish affair. There was a tremendous amount in it for me. But after my experience during the hymn I began to realise that God actually wanted to use me to help others. I began to search for the anointing and gifting needed to lead unbelievers to Christ.

In my early twenties while still at the same church, I joined the Scripture Union book club.[1] Every month I received a Christian book—sometimes teaching, sometimes testimony—and I always managed to finish it before the next one arrived. One month a book was delivered about teaching myself to speak in tongues, at least that was how it came over to me. It's actual title was *The Holy Spirit and You* by Dennis and Rita Bennett.[2]

I tried it—on my own in the bedroom when the house was empty—but I didn't dare tell anyone else, especially those at church. After three months of trying I thought I could manage two words. At least they didn't sound like English or French so I hoped they might be the real thing. After a year there were about six.

During this time I began speaking at some youth meetings and to my utter amazement several teenagers sought me out to make a commitment to Jesus Christ. One especially blessed gathering occurred after I tried singing in tongues while driving there. When I arrived, God seemed to give me the right words to say to the young people.

Eighteen months later, I went for an interview at St John's Theological College in Nottingham and attended a seminar given by a junior lecturer. He explained how signs and wonders were needed to accompany the Exodus event and the Jesus event but were no longer necessary in our present age. 'This is why signs and wonders do not happen today,' he said firmly. Afterwards, Michael Green, the principal, interviewed me and asked if I could speak in tongues.

'I don't think so,' I replied cautiously. This was partly due to the lecture I had heard and partly due to my own lack of confidence in what I was doing. Michael met my hesitancy with his own uncertainty and only agreed to take me on a year's probation. After the year was over, however, he was away in South Africa and the vice principal gave me permission to stay, as long as I behaved myself.

In my second year at college the junior lecturer had left and I was allowed to attend a charismatic Anglican church in the city. For the very first time I heard someone else speaking in tongues. Mine's not so bad after all, I thought to myself, and from then on the language began to flow more freely.[3]

As well as tongues I experienced more moments like the one in Egham church, some real tears and a prophecy or two which seemed right and helpful. But what really came across to me was the life, the expectancy of the people, the full church and the love they showed to one another and to me. Prior to this my Christianity had been something of an individual and private thing except for preaching. Now I realised there was enormous value in the body of Christ. For me learning to trust was a very slow process.

Looking back I can now see why this was so. At fourteen the world felt like a bad place and the people in it seemed to be bad news. My individual saviour met all my needs and talked with me alone in my bedroom. If I had God I didn't need people. I am so grateful that the first charismatic fellowship I ever encountered was a loving one. They began to teach me the importance of the body of Christ both from Scripture and from experience, and the large church was often full. People in the area regularly came to know the Lord.

When I became a vicar I wanted a charismatic church like the one in Nottingham. I wanted things to happen like they had for Dennis Bennett in Seattle, David Watson in York and Colin Urquhart in Lewsey.[4] Each of these three leaders experienced signs and wonders in their ministries and seemed to receive sizeable congregations as a result. The problem was I didn't know what to do and nobody would tell me. 'There's no blueprint,' people would say. 'No method.' Believing that I had met Jesus at the cross and wanting to serve him, I still did not know how to go any further.

David Watson's book *You Are My God* came out and I raced through it in a couple of days trying to find an answer. 'It doesn't say how he did it,' I moaned to my wife Carol.[5]

'Yes it does,' she said. 'David preached about speaking in tongues.' While I was in Nottingham I dated charismatic Carol and she has ever since encouraged and accompanied me in my search to discover more of God.

'Oh,' I said. 'I must have missed that bit.' So I preached about speaking in tongues. One young lady went home that night, asked for the gift and a beautiful language inspired by the Holy Spirit flowed from her lips. But she was the only one and nothing else happened.

Between 1984 and 1986 John Wimber came to England with his 'Signs and Wonders' conferences. I was not the only Anglican clergyman to be impressed. Unlike other American visitors he did not shout at us and in particular he did not shout at sick people, telling them to have more faith if they wanted to be healed. He taught us to invite the Holy Spirit to come and then watch to see what the Father was doing. The church he pastored was also full to overflowing.[6]

His theology was based on the works of academic scholars such as George Eldon Ladd on the kingdom and James D.G. Dunn on the Holy Spirit. This was strange to me because Ladd's book, first published in 1964, was a basic text book at our theological college while Jimmy Dunn was one of my lecturers at Nottingham University. I suppose I failed to connect their theology with signs and wonders because our examinations were theoretical and not practical. We always spent our time discussing what happened 'back there' and never thought much about its relevance for today.[7]

I came away from the conferences, reread the books and then turned to Scripture for myself. I especially wanted to ask about the coming of the kingdom of God. This is what I discovered.

The Kingdom of God

'In those days John the Baptist came, preaching in the Desert of Judea and saying, "Repent, for the kingdom of heaven is near" ' (Mt 3:2).

John the Baptist began his ministry by saying the kingdom of God was near.[8]

'After John was put in prison, Jesus went into Galilee, proclaiming the good news of God. "The time has come," he said. "The kingdom of God is near. Repent and believe the good news!" ' (Mk 1:14–15).

Jesus began his ministry by saying the kingdom of God was near.

'These twelve Jesus sent out with the following instructions: ... "As you go, preach this message: 'The kingdom of heaven is near' " ' (Mt 10:5,7).

The twelve Apostles began their ministry by saying the kingdom of God was near.

'After this the Lord appointed seventy-two others and sent them two by two ahead of him to every town and place where he was about to go. He told them, ... "When you enter a town and are welcomed, eat what is set before you. Heal the sick who are there and tell them, 'The kingdom of God is near you' " ' (Lk 10:1–2, 8–9).

The seventy-two began their ministry by saying the kingdom of God was near.

John the Baptist, Jesus, the twelve Apostles and the seventy-two all began by saying the kingdom of God was near. So when did it arrive? When did the kingdom of God move from being near to being here?

Jesus said, 'But if I drive out demons by the Spirit of God, *then* the kingdom of God has come upon you' (Mt 12:28, my italics). The kingdom of God comes when the Holy Spirit comes, kicking out the kingdom of darkness and bringing in the kingdom of light.

The kingdom of God which is 'near' is a reign not a realm. If the kingdom of God were a realm—an area, a place, a geographical location—then Jesus' kingdom would belong to this world (Jn 18:36), and the coming of the King into this world to establish his throne here would bring in his kingdom. But Jesus said, 'The kingdom of God does not come visibly, nor will people say, "Here it is," or "There it is," because the kingdom of God is within you' (Lk 17:20–21).

The kingdom of God is a reign. It has not come because the King is here but because the Holy Spirit is here. He comes to all who believe in Jesus. Jesus said, 'You know him, for he lives with you and will be in you' (Jn 14:17). This fits in with the prophecy of John the Baptist. 'I baptise you with water, but he will baptise you with the Holy Spirit' (Mk 1:8). That is why John said the kingdom of God was near. Not because Jesus had come—but because Jesus had come to baptise with the Holy Spirit. This is also why the twelve and the seventy-two, given power and authority, could do the same signs as the king. If the kingdom came with the king, then only the king would be able to do the signs. The result and Jesus' response were very revealing.

'The seventy-two returned with joy and said, "Lord, even the demons submit to us in your name." He replied, "I saw Satan fall like lightning from heaven" ' (Lk 10:17–18). The disciples of Jesus, given power and authority, can also pull down the kingdom of darkness and begin building the kingdom of light. Just as Satan was defeated in heaven, so he is now being defeated on earth, and because Jesus is the baptiser in the Holy Spirit, all who believe in him can continue to do the same.

'I tell you the truth, anyone who has faith in me will do what I have been doing. He will do even greater things than these, because I am going to the Father.... And I will ask the Father, and he will give you another Counsellor to be with you for ever—the Spirit of truth' (Jn 14:12,16). Jesus seems to see this coming of the Spirit of truth in power to his disciples as the coming of the kingdom of God.

'And he said to them, "I tell you the truth, some who are standing here will not taste death before they see the kingdom of God come with power" ' (Mk 9:1).

Jesus' final words before his ascension, after one of the twelve has already tasted death, confirms previous prophecies. 'Do not leave Jerusalem, but wait for the gift my Father promised, which you have heard me speaking about. For John baptised with water, but in a few days you will be baptised with the Holy Spirit.... You will receive power when the Holy Spirit comes on you' (Acts 1:4–5,8).

On the day of Pentecost the Holy Spirit came with power and is now available to all who believe in Jesus. 'Peter replied, "Repent and be baptised, every one of you, in the name of Jesus Christ so that your sins may be forgiven. And you will receive the gift of the Holy Spirit. The promise is for you and your children and for all who are far off—for all whom the Lord our God will call" ' (Acts 2:38–39).

Paul relates this to the kingdom of God. 'For the kingdom of God is not a matter of eating and drinking, but of righteousness, peace and joy in the Holy Spirit' (Rom 14:17). Paul also mentions the power. 'For the kingdom of God is not a matter of talk but of power' (1 Cor 4:20).

The coming of the Spirit of God with power to all who believe in Jesus is the coming of the kingdom of God. Whenever we pray, 'Your kingdom come' in the Lord's Prayer (Mt 6:10), we are in effect praying, 'Come, Holy Spirit.'

Those who receive him enter the kingdom of God. Jesus said, 'I tell you the truth, unless a man is born of water and the Spirit, he cannot enter the kingdom of God. Flesh gives birth to flesh, but the Spirit gives birth to spirit. You should not be surprised at my saying, "You must be born again" ' (Jn 3:5–7).

The Spirit of Jesus knocks at the door of our lives. If we let him in then the kingdom of God is within us. We become temples of the Holy Spirit (1 Cor 6:19). From then on, when we let God do what he wants to do in and through us by his Spirit, we are making Jesus the King of our lives. When this happens the kingdom of God is coming on earth as it is in heaven.

This is the Gospel of Jesus Christ. This Jesus who proclaimed the kingdom of God, healed the sick and cast out demons; who died for our sins on the cross, and defeated death by rising again and ascending into heaven; now pours out his Holy Spirit on us—that we may continue his work here on earth. It is the work of throwing out the kingdom of darkness and bringing in the kingdom of light.

James D.G. Dunn writes, 'The...kingdom was present for Jesus only because the...Spirit was present in and through him.... In other words, it was not so much a case of "Where *I* am there is the kingdom", as, "Where the *Spirit* is there is the kingdom". It was the manifestation of the power of God, which was the sign of the kingdom of God.'[9]

If this is right then the coming of the Holy Spirit, the coming of the kingdom of God to those who believe in Jesus is not an optional extra to Christianity, it is Christianity. Similarly the signs of that coming kingdom are not optional either, they are part of it. Signs of the kingdom are to the coming of the Holy Spirit what smoke is to fire. They are not optional and they are not separate. There is no smoke without fire.

As well as thinking through the theology I also put into practice what John Wimber had taught us at the conference. I began inviting the Holy Spirit to come among us and do whatever he wanted to do. Ever since then we have, from time to time, experienced some of the power of God, which is a sign of his kingdom.

One Tuesday evening I looked out over the very Anglican congregation which had come together for an official diocesan course. Most of them were standing, heads up, eyes closed, hands held out. One of them was definitely not. He stood on the edge of a row with his arms firmly folded across his broad chest and his eyes wide open staring straight at me. He looked like an ancient castle surrounded by a deep moat with the portcullis securely shut. I imagined he was repeating in his mind again and again, 'Over my dead body.'

The diocesan renewal group had set me up. Some of the older clergy had flown the charismatic flag for many years and now felt it was time for one of the younger chaps to have a go. So here I was trying to walk through treacle. I asked the Holy Spirit to come on these dear souls and to my mind God seemed to be struggling with them as much as we were. Virtually nothing appeared to be happening.

I then made a blunder. In my mind I said something to God which I ought not to have said. Indicating the stone statue at the end of the pew, I commented in my mind, 'Lord, not even you could move that guy.' I regretted it the moment the words were out, but it was too late.

In my time I have seen a number of people go over in the power of the Spirit. Laity normally fall backwards while clergy often go forwards on their faces. God seems to like it that way. Prior to this moment I had never seen anyone fall sideways.

Suddenly, without any warning, the man standing next to the conscientious objector crashed over sideways taking his neighbour with him. They became entangled with one another like professional wrestlers and rolled in the aisle with great togetherness. Eventually the British fortress freed himself, rose to his feet, dusted himself down, folded his armed even more firmly and resumed his original position. I didn't dare look at him any more.

Nothing else occurred. People began to sit down. The clock moved on to 9.30 pm which was our agreed finishing time. I said a closing prayer and dismissed the meeting. No one left. They all just sat there. 'You can go,' I repeated, 'that's it.' But nobody did.

After a few minutes' silence, which seemed like hours, the man who went down sideways and knocked the castle over spoke up. 'I think the Lord wants to anoint a number of people with the gift of healing,' he said.

At that moment I would have been grateful for anything. 'Right,' I responded. 'All those who'd like to be anointed for healing please come out to the front.' About fifty of the hundred present responded and gathered on the platform area beside the Lord's table. I asked the other half-dozen or so clergy who were present to hold up their hands like policemen on traffic duty and once more I prayed, 'Come, Holy Spirit.'

Almost immediately, all but three were poleaxed and ended on the floor. They were soon up and laid hands on the others who then also went over. This was a strange experience because everyone was back on their feet very quickly. All we can say is that sometimes when we invoke the Holy Spirit, the kingdom of God comes in power.

We believe it was the kingdom of God which came that night because of the difference the experience made to us and the signs which followed. For many who were present, including myself, it was the start of believing in the power of God to come and change lives. We did a number of courses together after this and many of the things which occurred have been recorded in my first two books. We attended those courses because we had experienced the signs of God's power that night. To God be all the glory.[10]

Sometimes, I think, there is confusion about the kingdom of God because what I have described is seen in the New Testament as the first of two comings. We live in the age when God is among us by his Spirit in an unseen way.

The kingdom at present can only be seen by faith and entered by faith. 'The secret of the kingdom of God' is given to Jesus' disciples but not 'to those on the outside' (Mk 4:11). It is like good seed sown in a field (Mt 13:24), or a planted mustard seed (Mt 13:31), or treasure hidden in a field. 'The kingdom of God is within you' (Lk 17:21).

But it will not always be like that. In the New Testament a second coming of the kingdom of God is also described.

> When the Son of Man comes in his glory, and all the angels with him, he will sit on his throne in heavenly glory. All the nations will be gathered before him, and he will separate the people one from another as a shepherd separates the sheep from the goats. He will put the sheep on his right and the goats on his left.
>
> Then the King will say to those on his right, 'Come, you who are blessed by my Father; take your inheritance, the kingdom prepared for you since the creation of the world' (Mt 25:31–34).

This is the second coming of the kingdom which will come when the King comes. There will be nothing hidden or secret about it. It will be a realm as well as a reign. 'All the nations of the earth . . . will see the Son of Man coming on the clouds of the sky, with power and great glory' (Mt 24:30). 'Every eye will see him' (Rev 1:7). This time it is the angels who will proclaim the coming kingdom 'with a loud trumpet call'; 'they will gather his elect from the four winds' (Mt 24:31).

According to the New Testament, the first coming of the kingdom of God is the coming of the Holy Spirit. The second coming of the kingdom is the coming of Jesus as King in glory. The first prepares for the second and we now live in this time of preparation. The birth, life, death, resurrection and ascension of Jesus make it possible for the kingdom of God to come today by his Spirit. We enter the kingdom by believing in Jesus, repenting of our sins, nailing our colours to the cross in baptism and receiving the Holy Spirit. We advance the kingdom by asking Jesus again and again to fill us with more and more of his Spirit that we may do the work of God and defeat the work of Satan.

This is important. Jesus did not send us out just to offer free tickets to heaven, nor did he tell us to abandon this world. He gave us power and authority to pull down the strongholds of Satan and to preach the good news of Jesus in order that the kingdom of God may come in and begin changing lives. When the Spirit comes bringing in the kingdom there will always be signs of his coming. When his fire burns within us others will see the smoke. We can do what Jesus did because the coming of the kingdom of God for the first time is the coming of the Holy Spirit, who is with us as he was with Jesus. I believe it is this theology of the kingdom of God which provides the basis for a ministry accompanied by signs.

After John Wimber's conferences we began asking God the Father, through Jesus, to send his Holy Spirit. Just as God promised in Luke 11:13, the Holy Spirit came again and again. How do we know he came? By the signs of his kingdom which accompanied his coming. Now I know how to begin doing the works of God. We ask the Father, through Jesus, to send his Holy Spirit upon us and wait for him to come. He normally comes most powerfully when the portcullis is up and the drawbridge is down.

Can we really expect signs as well as blunders in our particular congregations? The New Testament and much modern-day experience from churches where the Holy Spirit is welcome seem to suggest we can. There is also evidence today linking successful evangelism and an abundance of church growth with accompanying signs of the kingdom. But there can be dangers if we seek the signs rather than the kingdom.

Endnotes

1. Unfortunately the Scripture Union book club no longer exists.
2. Dennis and Rita Bennett, *The Holy Spirit and You* (Kingsway: Eastbourne, 1971).
3. Bill Subritzky teaches that spiritual gifts often start in the flesh, meaning naturally, and end in the spirit, meaning supernaturally. I suspect this is what may have happened with me and the gift of speaking in tongues.
4. The story of Dennis J. Bennett is told in his book, *Nine o'Clock in the Morning* (Coverdale House Publishers: Eastbourne, 1971).

   What happened to David Watson at York is recorded in his book, *You Are My God* (Hodder and Stoughton: London, 1983).

   Colin Urquhart's story is published in his book *When the Spirit Comes* (Hodder and Stoughton: London, 1974).
5. David Watson, *op cit*.
6. Much of John's teaching at those conferences can be found in his two books *Power Evangelism* (Hodder and Stoughton: London, 1985) and *Power Healing* (Hodder and Stoughton: London, 1986).
7. George Eldon Ladd, *Jesus and the Kingdom* (SPCK: London, 1966).

   James D.G. Dunn, *Baptism in the Holy Spirit* (SCM Press: London, 1970).

   James D.G. Dunn, *Jesus and the Spirit* (SCM Press: London, 1975).
8. Matthew's use of the term 'kingdom of heaven' is generally agreed by scholars to be synonymous with Mark and Luke's use of the term 'kingdom of God'. Matthew's use of the semitic idiom would be less meaningful to the Greek ear. Matthew wrote for Jews; Mark and Luke seem to have had a wider audience in mind.
9. James D.G. Dunn, *Jesus and the Spirit*, pp 48–49, op cit.
10. Peter H. Lawrence, *The Hot Line* (Kingsway Publications: Eastbourne, 1990).

    Peter H. Lawrence, *Doing What Comes Supernaturally* (Kingsway Publications: Eastbourne, 1992).

CHAPTER

4

Seek First the Kingdom of God

In a land of cities and towns where very few people know one another and keep themselves to themselves, evangelism and church-life usually suffer accordingly. A few years ago a survey of the world's main countries and their religious habits revealed that England was the second most godless nation on earth. Japan came first. A more recent MARC survey showed the Anglican churches in the Birmingham area to be some of the worst attended in the country. And—whenever the Christian leaders came together in the eighties to pray for Birmingham—they always spent some time praying for the spiritual desert of East Birmingham. This meant we were trying to minister at the agreed centre of spiritual barrenness in one of the hardest cities of the second most godless nation on earth. I heard recently that the normal Sunday attendance for a Protestant church in East Birmingham is only twenty people, compared to the West Midlands average of 122.[1]

One day we thought it was time to do something about it. The Spirit of God had begun moving powerfully among us so we thought maybe we could use this power to help some outsiders to become insiders; to know the presence of God's love; to find identity as children of God, and to join the community of Christian believers. We were convinced that we had some good news to offer. Power was what we needed and power was what seemed to have come to us. We had witnessed a policeman falling under the power of the Holy Spirit in our church and rising to his feet later as a believer.[2] It seemed now was the time to have a go at the opposition and tackle the criminals who breed well in their East Birmingham habitations of desolation.

During the night our local youngsters smashed cars and stole video-recorders from people's homes. During the day, whenever they were not asleep, we sought to befriend them. In our naivety we made many blunders.

Some Christian students from various countries came among us to help with the evangelistic work in the parish. They chatted with our new friends about Jesus and invited them for an evening to the church hall where the male members of the team slept.

The meeting went better than expected. Who said the local mafia were difficult to reach with the gospel? After some food, a Christian video and a personal challenge, several young people went into the kitchen to talk further about becoming Christians. They occupied the male members of the team for some time. When the enquirers came out their friends had gone; so had all the students' bags, musical instruments, passports and money.

Discouraged but not defeated, we tried to form them into a weekly youth club using the same hall. One evening a new member thought it would be rather fun to try and kill someone. He took a concrete slab and balanced it precariously over the door of the gents' loo. Fortunately the first person who entered reacted quickly and the slab only grazed him on its way to the floor.

We met on Friday evenings. When the club meeting ended we unleashed the criminal power we had gathered together on the unsuspecting neighbourhood. One artistic youth covered the local school wall with a magnificent mural done entirely with cans of spray paint. It cost the authorities several thousand pounds to remove it. I had a good relationship with the local headmaster before this happened.

Another teenager decided to settle into the local public phone-box for the night. In due course a lady came to use it, realised he was messing about and began banging on the window. At first he ignored her but eventually opened the door and popped his head out.

'Yes?' he enquired.

'I want the phone,' she shouted.

'Oh,' he replied in a very laid-back and much calmer manner than the lady. 'Why didn't you say so before?'

Slowly and deliberately the Christ Church youth member took out his Stanley knife, which he took everywhere with him, cut the cord and handed the telephone to the lady outside.

'Here you are, missus,' he said. 'Sorry to keep you waiting.'

The police asked us to close the club. They could handle our members in twos and threes, but we were organising them into twenties and thirties. Gangs who ran riot through the district after we kicked them out on a Friday night were not welcomed by the local constabulary.

So we started taking them in small groups to the most powerful charismatic meetings we could find. At one gathering in the North the minister laid hands on people one at a time as they knelt before the altar. Everyone went over in the power of the Holy Spirit. Everyone that is except our gang. Nothing happened to them. So they went to the back of the queue and tried again. The unsuspecting leader put his hand on their foreheads once more but with the same result.

We took them to hear John Wimber in London. They

heard a good sermon, saw God's power move among the people and heard the challenge to receive Jesus themselves. Right out of the blue Gene said to me. 'I'm going to have one more smoke then I'll ask Jesus to come into my life.' Sure enough he lit a cigarette, waited until there was nothing left and then prayed out loud asking Jesus to come into his life.[3]

On the way home he said to me, 'Peter, will you do me a favour?' 'Of course, Gene,' I said, willing at that point to do anything for our first convert. 'I'm in court on Tuesday,' he explained. 'Will you come and speak for me?'

I duly donned my clerical collar and jacket only to discover to my horror when I arrived at the Crown Court that Gene had been caught burgling the house two doors from where I lived. He was expected to go down for three years, but after I spoke he did only two months. He was delighted. The same local headmaster who heard what took place with one of his most troublesome former pupils was furious.

Undaunted, I took a car-full to another meeting in an Anglican church where the youngsters did their best to behave. Unfortunately they failed. If they went to the cinema or a football match they would naturally chat to their friends as it was taking place. They had never sat still and kept quiet in their lives. After a while it was too much for the lady church warden. She came up to them rather officiously and said, 'I'd like you to know I have the authority to throw you out of here.'

Yes, madam, I thought rather cynically to myself. You may have the authority, but I bet you don't have the power.

Neither did we. We sought power; we sought signs and wonders. We were new to this ministry and for a while it seemed like a game. We played by the rules we had learnt and believed we would be on the winning side. We expected great things to happen out on the street, as with

David Wilkerson and Nicky Cruz, but they never did. It was a painful time and I needed to face some difficult questions.[4]

Why was I really playing this game? Power? Success? Making friends and influencing people? I suspected it was all of that and more. I needed to come back to a few basic truths and think through the biblical approach to signs and wonders.

Seek first the kingdom of God

Jesus, full of the Holy Spirit, was tempted by Satan in the wilderness. 'If you are the Son of God' do these signs: turn stone into bread; jump from the highest point of the temple (Mt 4:3,5,6). He was offered 'all the kingdoms of the world' (Mt 4:8) as a reward. Jesus was tempted to do miracles—to see if he really was the Son of God. Seeking power and signs for their own sake belongs to the kingdoms of this world. Jesus said, 'A wicked and adulterous generation asks for a miraculous sign!' (Mt 12:39; 16:4). Paul encountered a similar problem. 'Jews demand miraculous signs,' he wrote, 'Greeks look for wisdom, but we preach Christ crucified' (1 Cor 1:22).

Those who are opposed to contemporary ministries of signs and wonders are not slow to quote these verses. They also go on to argue how such ministries may also be of the Devil. 'The coming of the lawless one will be in accordance with the work of Satan displayed in all kinds of counterfeit miracles, signs and wonders' (2 Thess 2:9). Similarly, the book of Revelation refers to 'spirits of demons performing miraculous signs' (Rev 16:14) and 'the false prophet who had performed the miraculous signs' (Rev 19:20).

There are, of course, other scriptures to set alongside these. John makes these comments: 'This the first of his miraculous signs, Jesus performed in Cana of Galilee. He thus revealed his glory, and his disciples put their faith in him' (Jn 2:11). 'After the people saw the miraculous sign that Jesus did, they began to say, "Surely this is the Prophet who is to come into the world" ' (Jn 6:14). 'Many in the crowd put their faith in him. They said, "When the Christ comes, will he do more miraculous signs than this man?" ' (Jn 7:31).

Three thousand were converted on the day of Pentecost when the Holy Spirit came in power (Acts 2); a number which grew to five thousand after Peter and John had been used to bring healing to the lame man (Acts 3 and 4).

Similarly, Paul himself can be placed on both sides of the fence. 'My message and my preaching were not with wise and persuasive words, but with a demonstration of the Spirit's power, so that your faith might not rest on men's wisdom, but on God's power' (1 Cor 2:4–5).

It is not, however, sufficient to throw one set of texts at our opponents as in a game of tennis without listening to the ones they throw back. '*All* scripture is God-breathed' (2 Tim 3:16, my italics).

In one incident recorded by John we have both sides of the argument coming together.

> When this man heard that Jesus had arrived in Galilee from Judea, he went to him and begged him to come and heal his son, who was close to death.
>
> 'Unless you people see miraculous signs and wonders,' Jesus told him, 'you will never believe.'
>
> The royal official said, 'Sir, come down before my child dies.'
>
> Jesus replied, 'You may go. Your son will live.'...
>
> So he and all his household believed (Jn 4:47–50, 53).

The answer seems to be that the royal official was not seeking signs and wonders, he only wanted his son to be healed. Jesus responds out of compassion, the boy recovers and the whole household believes. In contrast to worldly things, Jesus says, 'Seek first his kingdom and his righteousness, and all these things will be given to you as well' (Mt 6:33). And surely this is the solution. We do not seek signs for their own sake, for self-glory or spectacular power. We seek first the kingdom of God for his sake, his power and his glory. But when we seek to allow the Holy Spirit to come, to do what he wants us to do, there will inevitably be signs that follow and as a result some will believe.

Jesus said to his disciples:

> Go into all the world and preach the good news to all creation. Whoever believes and is baptised will be saved, but whoever does not believe will be condemned. And these signs will accompany those who believe: In my name they will drive out demons; they will speak in new tongues; they will pick up snakes with their hands; and when they drink deadly poison, it will not hurt them at all; they will place their hands on sick people, and they will get well (Mk 16:15–18).

The first coming of the kingdom, the coming of the Holy Spirit, is a foretaste of what is to come. He is 'a deposit guaranteeing our inheritance until the redemption of those who are God's possession' (Eph 1:14), 'guaranteeing what is to come' (2 Cor 5:5). The Holy Spirit comes to bring God's kingdom to the earth. In heaven all belong to God and worship him; no one is ill or dies; no fallen angels or demons are present. This is why he enables us to proclaim the kingdom, heal the sick and cast out demons. When we seek to do this by welcoming God among us, listening to his voice and obeying his call we are seeking first the kingdom of God. Biblical evidence suggests that when God's kingdom comes, signs of the kingdom will come with it—but it is the kingdom and not the signs which we seek.

On reflection I am now sure that I was seeking power and signs with which to impress the young people; I was not seeking first the kingdom of God. Without realising it I was trying to use Satan's methods to defeat Satan. Lucifer in his rebellion always seeks to match power with power. Unwittingly I had once more tried to rise very high instead of coming before God in weakness, humility and obedience at the foot of the cross.

I think our biggest blunder was rushing into an ill-conceived plan without spending enough time preparing and listening to God. When Jesus was given only three years in which to change the world he spent the first forty days alone with God in the desert.

I would like to say, having learnt my lesson, that I put it into practice straight away. What really happened was that God used humble Christians from our church to teach me the practical lessons. They were not particularly keen on miracles or power. They themselves had been saved by others loving them and sharing Jesus; they loved their friends and the people of the area and wanted the same for them. They had no bishop looking at confirmation numbers, size of congregation or amount of money on the plate; they were simply tired of Satan's kingdom dominating the area and sought instead to bring more people into God's kingdom. Their efforts proved to be a triumph of faith over experience and signs of God's love went with them.

One day four of them asked if they could go knocking on doors. I was not very encouraging. 'Do what you like,' I said, 'but it won't work. We've already tried it.'

I assumed they were going out on a sudden impulse, but unlike my attempts to reach the young people, much prayer, thought and planning came first. They talked to a number of people, listened to friends from the Birmingham City Mission and most especially listened to

God. In this way the Holy Spirit was invited to direct operations from the beginning. Our parish evangelism only began when those who had been praying believed they had received a God-given strategy.

The team began with Burney Lane, praying and pushing leaflets through letter-boxes which offered prayer for people's needs. Those who then returned the leaflets requesting prayer for anything or anyone received a call from a member of the evangelism group. Eventually all the houses were visited and a number of people were very warm and friendly. The team was welcomed into a number of homes. The problem came when they turned the corner and started work on Cotterills Lane.

The four evangelists persuaded others to go with them one evening and prayer-walk the street. Out loud in various groups they prayed for the people who lived there and asked the Lord to bind up the principalities and powers. They always saw spiritual warfare as an important and necessary task to tackle before seeking to advance God's kingdom. Once this was done they pushed leaflets prayerfully through every door, saying that people from Christ Church would be visiting soon to ask a few questions about God and the church. Then—armed with questionnaires and Christ Church badges—they went door-knocking.

This time they met opposition head-on. The natives were definitely not friendly. Rejection and different kinds of abuse came their way. So—they all met together and prayed again. 'Try the other side,' God seemed to say. Until that point the team had only visited houses on one side of the lane. They crossed over and tried again. Others were praying as they went.

Some people chatted to them on the doorstep for up to two or three hours. At other places they were invited inside. When asked if they would like to talk further about God some reacted positively. The team enlisted others to follow them up and after a while a little house group was formed. The newcomers responded well to the love of God which was shown to them.

While I was away the group had another prayerful idea: an evangelism service in August. Now everyone knows you don't hold an evangelism service in Birmingham during August. People do not come to Birmingham for their holidays: they go away to the seaside. The place is deserted. But they prayed and went for it. I believe it is now known as a 'seeker-friendly service'. The team put the title 'an informal service' on the leaflet which went into every house in Cotterills Lane.[5]

People prayed. The church was full. The visiting clergyman from Canada preached and thirteen came forward to make a commitment to Jesus Christ. We did it again in November and I preached. Another six came forward and in the following June sixteen adults were confirmed into the Christian church. What they saw, heard and experienced for themselves when they came among us were signs of God's kingdom.

I asked the Holy Spirit to come on them and several were physically shaken, warmed with love or slipped gently to the floor. The appropriate action at the right time for each person. Some demons manifested and needed attention. Everyone eventually felt very blessed.

Our little team of door-knockers were not seeking power or success. Compassion for the lost had merely risen within them and guided them down the lane of obedience. The prayer constantly on their lips was, 'Lord help us to do what you are blessing.' I have been humbled by their efforts and grateful to God for the way he has used and led them. The Spirit came and directed operations and led some local people to join us. When they mixed with us and experienced God's presence for themselves they too chose to enter the kingdom of God. Since I first began to write this down, two more families have come to know the Lord.

I had a phone call from prison the other day. The

chaplain arranged it. It was on behalf of a former member of our youth club who had become a guest of Her Majesty. I visited him at Christmas-time. He was attending regular Bible studies and learning to read better. Two others in different prisons have also contacted me and asked for copies of my books. I still pray for them and for East Birmingham. I suspect God has not finished with them yet.

The Holy Spirit helps us to build communities on earth which begin to resemble the kingdom of God in heaven. The Holy Spirit sends us out to compel people to come in and join the feast. This means that ministry to believers and mission to the world are both very important. Jesus and his disciples did both.

From time to time Christians have criticised us for spending so much time praying with Christians, believing we should be outside the sanctuary evangelising at every opportunity. The new General of the Salvation Army answered this recently on the radio when he said that his aim was to save people from the hell of this life as well as the hell to come in the next. This is kingdom theology. How can people believe in a kingdom of God that is yet to come if there is no sign of it here on earth? How can people believe in a supernatural God who is spirit if there is no evidence of a supernatural God at work among us by his Spirit? How can people believe at all if no one goes out to tell them where the feast is being held? Ministry to Christians and mission to the world are crucial. They are complementary ingredients of the same gospel.

Kjell Sjoberg writes:

> As society becomes more and more godless, the Church must increasingly see itself as, and in practice structure itself deliberately to become, a counter-culture. This is necessary to enable the Church to be true to the Gospel and its prophetic role in the world.... The Lord calls and continues to call out a new society

> of persons unconditionally committed to exchanging the values of the surrounding society for the standards of Jesus' kingdom.... Thus the prophetic and evangelistic dimensions of the Gospel are totally interwoven with the life and witness of the community of the King.[6]

It is our experience that regularly inviting Father God through Jesus to send his Holy Spirit has brought more of his kingdom upon us. At times we have heard his voice, felt his love, seen his power and been led to share the good news with our neighbours. But it has not always been comfortable. Sin, evil and demons have been exposed along with the root causes of bad relationships and some sicknesses. We have not always tackled these successfully. Sometimes our church has appeared to be in an awful mess and many problems are still with us, but in a strange way this has held its own attraction for those with problems. If there is one thing the Spirit has done more than anything else at Burney Lane it is to take away the masks, the barriers of superficiality and the desire to pretend to be what we are not. This is not yet heaven, but there are signs of God's kingdom which suggest we have begun on the right path, and this reality gives hope to those in need.

John the Baptist said that Jesus would 'baptise...with the Holy Spirit and with fire' (Mt 3:11). When we light a bonfire in the garden we do so in order to burn rubbish, but our neighbours will know about it because of the smoke sign which goes with it. When we seek first the kingdom of God and allow the Holy Spirit to burn away our rubbish, it is my belief that our neighbours will know about that too because of the signs of God's grace which come whenever he comes.

It is a wicked and adulterous people who seek signs. We seek first the kingdom of God and trust that God's signs will come when the kingdom comes. The signs of

God's kingdom help us to know when it is here. It is therefore important that we can identify these signs—to know when it is God's kingdom which is being advanced. We need to look next at the kind of signs we can expect when God's kingdom comes upon us in the power of the Holy Spirit.

Endnotes

1. Unfortunately I cannot remember the details of the earlier survey, but the booklet *Prospects for the Nineties* gives information about trends and tables from the English Church Census.
   Peter Brierley, *Prospects for the Nineties* (MARC Europe: London, 1991).
2. This particular policeman is, as I write, the church warden at Christ Church, Burney Lane.
3. I think this was a day conference with John Wimber held at the Wembley Indoor Arena in 1987.
4. David Wilkerson, *The Cross and the Switchblade* (Marshall Pickering: London, 1963).
5. The Willow Creek Church in Chicago have pioneered work on 'Seeker Targeted' and 'Seeker Friendly' services. Grove Books have produced a helpful booklet on the subject and CPAS have done a workbook which may be photocopied. We found both very helpful.
   Paul Simmonds, *Reaching the Unchurched* Grove Booklets on Evangelism, no. 19 (Grove Books Limited: Bramcote, Notts., 1992).
   Anne Hibbert, *Creating a Church for the Unchurched* (CPAS: Warwick, 1992).
6. Kjell Sjoberg, *The Prophetic Church* (New Wine Press: Chichester, 1992), pp 19–20.

CHAPTER

5

On Earth as in Heaven

When Peter, our church warden, left Birmingham and moved to Penzance I asked him to find us a place in Cornwall where some of us could stay for a holiday. It took him a little while but eventually he wrote to say he'd found somewhere; a bed, breakfast and evening meal establishment with a difference.

When I made this request, I never thought he would discover a site steeped in history going back to Earl Harold who had owned it prior to being slain at Hastings. I did not expect to be visiting a large country mansion with its own chapel, where King Charles I had been before me and where a copy of the world-famous equestrian painting of him, presented by his son to the Vyvyan family, still hangs in the hall. Little did I imagine the drive to the house would be more than a mile long, through acres of private woodland and grassy fields, where broad-tipped, feather-footed buzzards soar and swoop during the day and colonies of rabbits play at dusk. And even if I had dreamed of such a place, there is no way I would have anticipated that part of such a stately home would be run by former members of St Andrew's, Chorleywood as an ecumenical Christian centre for conference courses, retreats, away-days, weekends and holidays.[1]

But this is what Peter found: 'Trelowarren' on the southernmost peninsular of England where seals bob up and down in the sea and long-necked black cormorants skim the surface looking for food. Such was the holiday residence for our little renewal group.[2]

We arrived on Saturday and the following morning I presided at Holy Communion for both residents and visitors in the chapel. On Monday evening our small group gathered together in the large drawing-room where another painting attributed to Van Dyke looked down on us. In 1644 King Charles I conferred a Baronetcy on Richard Vyvyan whose portrait hangs in the room alongside one of his wife. The Vyvyan family still live in the private part of the house. Seated beside the large open fireplace, where logs burn continually in the winter, Vivian, a local farmer, told us his story.

> In September 1986 my right hip gave out as I turned suddenly while walking along. At the time I felt fit and strong having always enjoyed good health, but when it didn't get any better I went to see my doctor. I was sent for X-rays which confirmed that I had spondylosis of the lower spine—premature wearing of the vertebrae. Physiotherapy helped a little but I was told to avoid lifting, bending and tractor-driving.
>
> I carried on farming for three years despite increasing pain in my lower back and hips which at times was almost unbearable. In the autumn of 1989 I felt further pains in my upper arms and neck and more X-rays confirmed spondylosis in the upper spine. In effect this meant a vertebra at the top of the spine and one at the base were now disintegrating. By the summer of 1990 I was no longer able to work and we had to consider sub-letting the place where my father had been born in 1912.

The medical profession did their best. I went to a physiotherapist, chiropractor, osteopath and homeopathic doctor, but my condition continued to deteriorate. On November 5th 1991, a consultant examined me, looked at my X-rays, read my notes and then faced me with the truth. My hips and spine were in such a poor state that I was no longer fit to do even the lightest of work. I arrived home at about five o'clock feeling worse than ever before, finding even the walk from the garage to the house almost too painful to bear. I felt as if all hope had gone.

A week before, George, a retired farmer from the next village had asked me if I would go with him to a service of Christian healing at Trelowarren on November 5th. I had said, 'Yes', but after the consultant's hammer blow I no longer felt like going. I told my wife, Jill, I would still go but wished the family was coming with me.

Our daughter, Rebecca, aged sixteen, heard this and asked if I really believed Jesus could heal me. I turned away. I couldn't answer. I'd been a church-goer all my life and had made my own profession of faith in Christ, but this was different. Rebecca asked me again and I knew I needed to give an answer. I turned to my family and found myself saying, 'Yes, I really do.'

The place is special but the people even more so. I felt such love among everyone there that I was released into praising God in a way I had never done before. I felt very weak and in pain, but as I praised him with all that I had, I knew it would be right to go forward for prayer.

As David, the warden of Trelowarren, called people forward, he added that some people might still not be quite sure about God. 'God is a God of love,' he added and I felt an unknown barrier lifting from me. It was still painful trying to stand and walk to the front, but two men called me forward and sat me in a chair. The power of the worship left me too emotional to tell them much about myself, but with one at my side and one at my feet they prayed for me in the name of Jesus.

When I awoke the next morning I felt like new. I told my family I was healed. Our son, Timothy, aged thirteen, responded immediately, 'Dad,' he began, 'we knew if you went Jesus would make you well again.'

After Jill went to work and the children to school, Vivian worked all day long. When they returned home there was a large trailer over-laden with firewood which he had cut and stacked. Jill was utterly amazed.

Three weeks later the doctor could find nothing wrong, then saw him after another month and told him not to come back. Another month later the surprised physiotherapist gave Vivian a thorough examination and said he was like 'a new one'. He returned to farming, rearing calves, making hay, driving tractors, harvesting corn and doing all the heavy lifting himself. In a letter to me later Vivian wrote: 'I shall never again be afraid to confess the faith in Christ crucified. Our lives have been completely turned upside down. Praise God.'

When the story was finished there was a deep, profound silence among those of us assembled around the fireplace. If God is active in the big toe of our country maybe there is hope for the rest of us.

This account thrilled us all but made life a little uncomfortable for me. I was due to speak and minister at the Trelowarren monthly healing service on the following evening. What could I teach them?

I returned home early from the beach mid-afternoon and asked God for help. He reminded me that Peter, my ex-church warden, who had suffered a heart attack earlier in the year, and two of my prayer partners, Kay and Beth, would be coming from Penzance. I smiled inwardly. Peter is a man full of faith; Kay and Beth had never prayed publicly for anyone in their lives. If all three were present this seemed to represent an acceptable way of proceeding.

As I stood on the landing next to King Charles, I noticed Peter's familiar bald head arriving. The chapel was packed. The overflow in the library was full. There were over 150 people present when I invited Peter to come forward. He told us all of a thrombosis he'd suffered the previous week and now his leg and ankle were badly swollen. He was grateful for the offer of prayer.

When I asked if Kay and Beth were present they were too near the front to hide or refuse my request. Kay went distinctly pale and silent while Beth mouthed how she was going to get me afterwards, but they both came forward and laid hands on Peter.

'Come, Holy Spirit,' I prayed into the microphone and then we all waited in silence. Gradually power came upon Peter. His bald head began to glow like a Belisha beacon. Slowly and quite gently his knees buckled and he went down on the floor. Kay and Beth made sure he was comfortable and continued laying hands on him.

After a short while Beth commented how his heart beat suddenly slowed down. A few minutes later Peter opened his eyes, was helped to his feet and felt much better. He said the swelling had now gone down and rolled up his trouser leg to show us the evidence. Two days later Peter phoned to say his leg was perfectly normal and the ankle which they had not been able to see for a week was now as clearly defined as the other one.

Vivian was also there that night with a friend called Richard who was suffering from spondylosis. Vivian and I laid hands on him and asked the Holy Spirit to come, and Richard experienced something similar to Peter. When Vivian wrote to me he said, 'Richard feels the Lord has healed him.' I am also pleased to say that Kay and Beth have now forgiven me.

God does love us and sometimes when his Holy Spirit comes upon us in power, people are healed. This is the

Spirit of Jesus. When Jesus was on earth he healed the sick. This is the end-time Spirit. When Jesus comes again there will be a new heaven and a new earth, but 'no more death or mourning or crying or pain, for the old order of things has passed away' (Rev 21:4). The Holy Spirit acts as a link between the first and second coming of Jesus. He confirms both and they confirm him.

We know Jesus healed the sick when on earth because the Spirit of Jesus heals the sick today. We know this is the Holy Spirit at work today because he does the same things that Jesus did as recorded in the Bible. We know there is a kingdom of God in heaven where there is no sickness and pain because when the Spirit of God comes in power today he often takes away sickness and pain. We know this is the same Holy Spirit because he gives us a taste now of the things Scripture promises we shall receive in full at the close of the age.

Healing is one of the signs of the kingdom. What we do and receive and taste now through the Holy Spirit is a foretaste of what is to come. Those who expect the signs of God's kingdom to be only made manifest in heaven ignore the doctrine of the Holy Spirit and his presence with us today. Those who expect everything we are promised in the New Testament to be ours today by faith go beyond the truths of scripture. The Holy Spirit gives us a taste of heaven but the best is yet to be.

After the description of the new heaven and the new earth the angel says to John, 'Do not seal up the words of the prophecy of this book, because the time is near. Let him who does wrong continue to do wrong; let him who is vile continue to be vile; let him who does right continue to do right; and let him who is holy continue to be holy' (Rev 22:10–11). For now the wheat and weeds live side by side (Mt 13:30) and 'we ourselves, who have the firstfruits of the Spirit, groan inwardly as we wait eagerly for our adoption as sons, the redemption of our bodies' (Rom 8:23). We can begin to taste heaven here and now, but we are not there yet. The coming of the Holy Spirit today is a foretaste and not the consummation of God's kingdom.

It is right that we should be careful with our expectations and not lead people with false hope. Our bodies still decay; we all still face physical death; sin, Satan and demons are still very much with us. But when the Spirit comes bringing in the kingdom, we begin to experience more of life 'on earth as it is in heaven'. Our experience of the Holy Spirit increases our faith in the scriptures and the truths of the Bible enable us to test our experience. The pictures of Revelation and the stories of Jesus in the gospels can help us to know what signs of the kingdom to expect when the Holy Spirit comes among us.

We have already seen how one sign of God's kingdom is healing. A second is the removal of evil.

There was no longer any sea

In the book of Revelation the sea represents evil from which came the blasphemous beast (Rev 13:1). In the new heaven and new earth there will be no more evil (Rev 21:1), no more Babylon, the home of demons (Rev 18:21), no more army of Satan (Rev 20:9), no more sinners (Rev 21:8; 22:15), no more beast and false prophet (Rev 20:10), no more death and Hades (Rev 20:14) and no more Satan (Rev 20:10). This is in keeping with the work of Christ when on earth. 'The reason the Son of God appeared was to destroy the devil's work' (1 Jn 3:8). From the desert, throughout his ministry, through the cross and resurrection, Jesus defeated Satan. He made it possible for us to be forgiven and cleansed from all evil (1 Jn 1:9).

When the Holy Spirit comes he convicts of sin (Jn 16:8–10), brings assurance of forgiveness and acceptance by God (Gal 4:6), and enables us to cast out demons (Mt 12:28). This is often the least comfortable part of God's coming among us. Sometimes within a few weeks of becoming Christians people will come and visit me. 'Peter,' they invariably say, 'it isn't working. Life has become much harder and I feel worse than before I was a Christian.' When they say this I know they have been truly converted.

The Holy Spirit has come to live inside them at their invitation and now they feel very uncomfortable with sin. Things they did before without thinking about them, sometimes without even knowing they were sins, now make them feel guilty—not right—upset and miserable. This is the coming of the kingdom of God, but it is vital at this point to confess, receive forgiveness, feel forgiven and where necessary have demons cast out. If these procedures are not followed we will have churches full of miserable sinners, but seeing it through can lead to freedom and joy.

Lisa (not her real name) formed a singing duo with her brother, acquired Equity cards and for nine years proved to be popular and successful on TV, radio and theatre. In 1979 she retired from show business and during her training as a nurse made a commitment to Jesus Christ. Lisa did not stop singing but helped every week with the church music group, that is until the beginning of November 1992 when she lost her voice!

At first, the medical profession told Lisa it was a virus and decided to let it run its course. When this failed to provide the desired effect they tried antibiotics in case there was some residual infection. After these drugs proved unsuccessful they gave antihistamine a whirl to overcome any allergic response there might be. All this time Lisa was told to use her voice as little as possible: but nothing worked. Finally she was referred to a surgeon as the only remaining medical explanation was polyps on the vocal cords.

In January 1993, while waiting for the referral, Lisa visited us at Christ Church, Burney Lane. The Holy Spirit came upon her quite powerfully several times at both the six and eight o'clock services. Lisa felt greatly blessed but not healed. The next morning Tanya and Christine from the church ministry teams saw her for a private session. This is Lisa's account of what happened:

> As they prayed with me Tanya felt led to command whatever had hold over my throat and my health in general to go. I became very aware of a fight going on inside me. I felt 'fear' but I wasn't frightened due to a very strong awareness of God's presence. Once I shared this the commands turned from general to specific. After continuing in this vein for a while my hands and arms both turned icy up to the elbow. The same happened with my knees but not with my feet. There is no physical explanation for this as I was seated in an easy chair with my hands relaxed in my lap.
>
> Another team member, Pat, arrived, and 'words' were given about problem areas. Most made sense and I could accept them.
>
> The 'fight' continued for some time until abruptly I began to feel better and an overwhelming peace took its place. Everything returned to normal other than a head which felt like a lump of mashed potato and the rest of me feeling as if I'd run a marathon.
>
> Much later, having pulled myself together, I set off on the motorway. The song 'El Shaddai' was going around in my head so I joined in and sang with it. Then I realised what I'd done; what had happened. I praised God in song all the way up the motorway and could still speak after over an hour's solid singing. I had been healed.

I am pleased to say that the healing remained and Lisa continued to speak clearly and sing without difficulty. No operation was needed. Sometimes when the Holy Spirit comes in power evil is exposed, tackled and removed. Then the kingdom of God has come among us.

Healing and the removal of evil are signs of God's kingdom but perhaps the most dramatic is the raising of the dead.

No more death

Raising people from the dead is a good example of the 'already' and 'not yet' tension which exists between the firstfruits of the kingdom which are 'already' being tasted and the best which is 'yet' to be.

Jesus says, 'He who believes in me will live, even though he dies; and whoever lives and believes in me will never die' (Jn 11:25–26). Jesus raised three people from the dead (Mt 9:18–26; Lk 7:11–17; Jn 11:1–44), and commanded the twelve he sent out to 'raise the dead'. Peter was used to raise Tabitha (Acts 9:40) and Paul did something similar with Eutychus (Acts 20:9–12). In the kingdom of God described in Revelation 21:4, 'there will be no more death'.

And yet it seems likely that Joseph died before Jesus (from the cross Jesus asks John to look after Mary), John the Baptist is executed, Judas hangs himself and three men died on Good Friday whom Jesus could not heal or save from physical death. Stephen becomes the first martyr, James dies by the sword while Peter is released from prison by an angel. All the members of the early church who were filled with the Holy Spirit are now dead.

Occasionally the Holy Spirit enables people to be raised from the dead. This is a taste of the kingdom of God which is yet to come where there will be no more death.

In November 1981, while living in South Africa, Mike and Linda attended a conference led by Bill Burnett, then the Archbishop of Cape Town. They were both filled with the Holy Spirit and began to speak in tongues.

The next day friends came to visit for a barbecue which

took place on the far side of the house. After finishing lunch the parents were talking so the children went off to amuse themselves. The adults assumed the older ones were looking after the younger ones not knowing someone had failed to close the door which led to the swimming pool. Quite unexpectedly a strange kind of hush came over the whole place. Linda sensed something was wrong. Suddenly there was a scream and instinctively they raced to the swimming pool.

Courtland, aged two-and-a-half, had been lying on the bottom of the pool for something like half-an-hour when the older children spotted him there. Linda is a trained Red Cross swimming instructor and knows there is very little time for oxygen to be withheld from the brain before damage and death occurs. She knew such time had long since passed.

The adults helped the other children to pull Courtland from the pool and laid him on the side. The little body was cold, grey, hard and clammy. Mike joined Linda but they could not get Courtland's mouth open to try resuscitation. Linda ran off to ring for help and said a very brave prayer. 'Lord take him or heal him completely.'

Mike eventually forced his little son's mouth open and for fifteen minutes tried breathing into him without any sign of success. They gave up for a short while. Linda returned and with Mike they prayed that God would restore Courtland to them. Mike began again and suddenly Courtland began to breathe. They wrapped him in a towel but there was no reaction coming from their son only a gurgling coming from his mouth. Linda has worked with brain-damaged children using swimming as a form of exercise therapy and she recognised that the most severely handicapped child she'd ever seen gave out this same sort of gurgling incoherent sound.

They took their little boy to the hospital and while the medical practitioners pumped the water out of his lungs Mike called their Anglican Vicar, Hugh, to ask for Bill and Sheila Burnett and the church to begin praying for Courtland's healing. Hugh took their elder son Matthew to the vicarage and then returned to the hospital.

The doctors came out with bad news. Courtland's temperature was rising and they were afraid of pneumonia. The church prayed for the temperature to go down. A little while later a doctor came out and became confrontational. He wanted the parents to go home. It was obvious they did not think Courtland was going to improve and were thinking of taking him off the machine which was aiding his breathing. Fortunately Hugh stepped in, saying they would wait and under no circumstances would they leave until they were ready to do so.

Much prayer, anxiety and feelings of guilt later, the temperature began to drop. Courtland was taken to the children's ward where Mike and Linda were allowed to see him. This is what Linda wrote down for me:

> He looked so still and quiet as we came into the ward. He was in a cot with white bed-clothes on. I remember leaning over and looking at him through the bars of the cot. I whispered his name. He sort of slightly moved his closed eyes. He just didn't talk I am sure from the suction and the dryness of his throat. Instead he held up his little hands to show us the old children's rhyme, 'Here is the church, here is the steeple. Open the door and see all the people.' This was a familiar game we played—God's signature was all over it. We knew, but knew, that God had saved him and healed him completely.

At six am the following morning, Mike and Linda were woken by the constant ringing of a phone which would not give up. It was urgent. It was the hospital. Would they please come and collect Courtland immediately as he was tearing up the nursery.

I played chess with Courtland a few years ago. A very

bright lad. In 1992 we met him again in California and went swimming with him in his Great Uncle's pool. It was a great joy to see how strong, athletic and comfortable he is in the pool. To God be all the glory.

I have taken the very sad funerals of a number of children during my ministry. Often their parents have prayed and their children have not been healed or raised from the dead. We cannot always understand God's ways but the restoring to life of Courtland by God is not discredited by other tragedies. Indeed it gives extra hope to bereaved parents. Every time God through Jesus in the power of the Holy Spirit raises someone from the dead our faith in Jesus as the 'resurrection and the life' is increased. There is no more death in heaven.

Physical healing, removing evil and raising the dead are all signs of the kingdom of God. So is emotional healing.

No more crying

This is a slightly more complex issue because, although there is no more crying or mourning in heaven, Jesus wept while on earth. Similarly, Paul encourages us to weep with those who weep. The really big boys do cry. Time and time again I have also seen the Holy Spirit help people to cry.

When Roger's mother died he was a mature adult but found he was unable to cry. The root of the problem seemed to go right back to his earliest days. His mother's first two children died soon after birth and she was advised not to have any more. So when Roger was born the specialist took him away and separated him from his mother for the first few months of his life. He survived physically but emotionally there were scars due to a lack of bonding with his parents in his formative months.

Some fifteen years after his mother died Roger received counselling and ministry. Demons were cast out and as the Holy Spirit came powerfully on him Roger began to cry. This brought a tremendous feeling of emotional release, greater freedom in Christ and something of a healed relationship with his mother even though she had died some time ago.

'No crying' in heaven is surely not a bottling-up of emotions but rather complete emotional healing to accompany the spiritual and physical wholeness already mentioned. The healing of past hurts is not always so easy to find in Scripture, but it is certainly a fact of heaven.

As well as tears Jesus also experienced the Holy Spirit releasing joy in him. 'At that time Jesus, full of joy through the Holy Spirit, said, "I praise you, Father, Lord of heaven and earth" ' (Lk 10:21).

On one occasion I invited the Holy Spirit to come on a group of about a hundred people. Almost immediately some started laughing. I tried not to show it, but I found this quite difficult to handle. The coming of God to his people is an awesome moment and not to be taken lightly. Fortunately I had seen this happen once or twice before at meetings and knew it could sometimes be of God.

I looked around trying to decide if people needed discipline or encouragement. One or two made me feel doubtful but one large man close to me gave a different impression. His eyes were closed, though watering with much laughter, but his countenance was beaming with a distinctly godly shine. I allowed it all to continue and after a while all kinds of different things began happening. Some fell; some shook; some wept; some were released into forgiveness. There were signs of much power and love.

Afterwards the man who was laughing near me told us about the still birth of his child a few weeks earlier. This was the first time he had felt emotional release over the tragedy and God did it through laughter.

This seemed very much to me like the foretaste of heaven where there will be no more crying because it will all have been done by then—nothing more to be worked through—complete wholeness in spirit, body and emotions. I believe the coming of the Holy Spirit often helps us to go further along that road. Physical, spiritual and emotional healing are all signs of the kingdom of God.

God sometimes heals the sick but the good news of heaven is not just an absence of negatives. There are some exciting things awaiting us as well.

God with us

' "The virgin will be with child and will give birth to a son, and they will call him Immanuel"—which means "God with us" ' (Mt 1:23). Matthew applies this Old Testament prophecy to Mary's son. Jesus himself said, 'Anyone who has seen me has seen the Father' (Jn 14:9).

While Jesus was on earth God was very much in the midst of his people. The same will be true in heaven. In Revelation 21:3 John writes: 'I heard a loud voice from the throne saying, "Now the dwelling of God is with men, and he will live with them. They will be his people, and God himself will be with them and be their God." '

Sometimes people say to me they are afraid of being in God's presence or even bored by the idea of it. I can only assume they do not know God. Before St Peter really knew Jesus he was afraid. As an expert fisherman he worked hard all night and caught nothing. Jesus told him where to fish and they caught so many that the boat began to sink. Peter's immediate response was, 'Go away from me, Lord; I am a sinful man' (Lk 5:8). Jesus told him not to be afraid.

Three years later a similar thing occurred (Jn 21:4–6). This time Peter's reaction is quite different. He leapt into the water and hurriedly made his way in the direction of Jesus. This is worth thinking about. The rush towards Jesus, rather than cowering away from him, was not because Peter had given up sinning since the last time; far from it. He had attempted murder, denied Jesus three times, run away and called down curses upon his head (Mt 26:69–75). I am not sure you can get much worse than this. The reason Peter ran towards Jesus and not away from him was because he now knew Jesus better. Not only was he unafraid of Jesus despite his own sin but he was positively excited by his presence.

This is why experiencing the Holy Spirit here and now is so important. He makes Jesus known. The Bible can help us to know about Jesus; the Holy Spirit helps us to know him personally. From the least to the greatest we can all know God, taste the thrill of his presence and hear his voice (Heb 8:11). 'But you know him, for he lives with you and will be in you' (Jn 14:17). 'And this is how we know that he lives in us: we know it by the Spirit he gave us' (1 Jn 3:24).

On one occasion as I was praying I began to see visions in my mind of people in the same weekly prayer-group as myself. Afterwards I shared them at our meeting. In one picture I saw Gill on top of a cliff. She was fitted with a hang-glider and wore a very safe harness. In the picture was a very large hand supporting her and holding the cord. I assumed this was the hand of God.

'Are you sure this is a good idea?' asked Gill.

'Yes,' replied God, 'You're OK.'

'Don't let go of the cord,' continued Gill a shade nervously.

'Go for it,' encouraged God.

Gill jumped off most beautifully and soon afterwards God let go of the cord. She flew high against the blue sky, round and round over the white cliffs supported only by the coastal winds. Eventually Gill glided down and made a competent landing on the beach.

'That was marvellous,' said Gill to God. 'But I'd never have managed it if you hadn't been holding the cord.'

Gill is a most competent Christian mum but often feels

weighed down with the routine and daily drudgery of life. Sometimes she feels guilty, as many Christian mums do, that she isn't praying or reading her Bible or witnessing more than she is. I believe God was saying he wanted Gill to have some non-religious fun, to let her hair down occasionally and know that God was with her.

Unknown to me, Gill and her husband Andy had seen some hang-gliders in the air while travelling during the holiday season. Three days before the prayer meeting at which I gave the message they had been discussing the practical possibilities of actually going hang-gliding. Gill said afterwards, 'I suppose generally we expect God to speak to us only about spiritual matters, but this showed he really cared about me and what I was doing.'

I think there are many more Christians who need to be told often—'God is with us.' Signs of the kingdom of God are to be expected. The norm for God's people as seen in the garden of Eden before the fall and as seen in the life of the sinless Jesus, is to be in communion with God. 'Words' of knowledge, 'words' of wisdom, 'words' of prophecy, even 'words' in a Spirit-language are all 'words' from God. They are signs that the broken relationship between God and his people has been restored through the blood of Jesus and the presence of the Holy Spirit. They are signs that the God who speaks is with us; he is in us.

Sometimes the Holy Spirit heals us in body, soul or spirit and sometimes he helps us to know the mind of Christ. These are all signs of God's kingdom but the main activity of heaven is worship.

Worship

When Jesus was on earth he worshipped. On the Sabbath day he went into the synagogue as was his custom (Lk

4:16). He also allowed others to worship him (Mt 2:11; 14:33; 28:9,17; Lk 24:52; Jn 9:38).

Worship also occupies the hosts of heaven.

> Day and night they never stop saying:
> 'Holy, holy, holy,
> is the Lord God Almighty,
> who was, and is, and is to come' (Rev 4:8).

The Holy Spirit enables us to begin doing this. He can take us from being singers of songs to being worshippers of God.

Danny Daniels is a man who has known deep sadness in his own life and yet his attitude to worship is one which I find to be very refreshing. In 1982 he attended a Zulu Assembly of God meeting in Soweto, South Africa where they worshipped God together for over two hours. Danny could not speak one word of their language. He did not know any of the songs nor recognise any of the music so he sang in tongues with them until they finished. He shared with me how it was a time of blissful togetherness worshipping in spirit. They sang in their native language and Danny sang in a spiritual tongue but all were united in worship by the Holy Spirit.[3]

Those who have tasted Spirit-filled worship often look forward to heaven where every God-given desire is satisfied. It is the desire of every human being from every culture to worship, whether it is a pop-star, a sports-star or a material possession. Such objects of worship will never meet our needs, however, because it is only one-way traffic. In heaven the desire to worship will be fully met because as we give worth to God so he gives worth to us.

Worship is affirmation one of another—drawing near to kiss. Our example is the Trinity. When the Holy Spirit came on Jesus a voice was heard to say, 'You are my Son, whom I love; with you I am well pleased' (Lk 3:22). On another occasion Jesus said, 'Father... glorify your Son, that your Son may glorify you' (Jn 17:1). Life, eternal life and the celebration of life expressed through worship, praise, adoration and thanks is for pleasure-seekers. When the Holy Spirit comes upon us giving great joy in worship then the kingdom of God is truly among us.

Spiritual healing, physical healing, emotional healing, experiencing God with us and enjoying his presence are signs of God's kingdom. When God's Spirit comes and these things begin to happen then we can be sure we are experiencing some of the benefits of Christ's passion here on earth as it is in heaven. They are the evidence of knowing God as Father through Jesus his son. Flowing from this new relationship with God can also come new relationships with one another, both religious and secular. Two important such healings are hinted at in the book of Revelation. 'I did not see a temple in the city, because the Lord God Almighty and the Lamb are its temple' (Rev 21:22).

I believe this means that there is no religion in heaven. The walls of our temples will be removed. There we shall see God face to face and have a living relationship with him. The religious barriers we erect between ourselves will be gone, and so will the political ones.

'On each side of the river stood the tree of life, bearing twelve crops of fruit, yielding its fruit every month. And the leaves of the tree are for the healing of the nations' (Rev 22:2). There will be no more religion in heaven and neither will there be any hunger, wars or rumours of wars. 'The wolf will live with the lamb' (Is 11:6); They will beat their swords into ploughshares and their spears into pruning hooks (Mic 4:3).

I am always thrilled when I hear of Christians giving to the needy of the world, at home and abroad. I am sure this is another sign of God's kingdom. Sometimes when the Spirit comes today we may also receive a degree of religious and political healing. I shall concentrate on religious and political healing in the following two chapters.

Endnotes

1. David and Vivien Viol are no longer the wardens at Trelowarren but the meetings and courses are still flourishing. Details can be obtained from: Trelowarren Fellowship, Mawgan-in-Meneage, Helston, Cornwall TR12 6AD.
2. 'Our little renewal group' was the East Birmingham Renewal Group to which I referred in Chapter One, and gave details in the endnotes.
3. Danny Daniels is a songwriter and worship leader who attends Crossroads Church in Denver, Colorado.

CHAPTER

6

No Religion in Heaven

When I was first invited to go to Ireland I was not at all keen. It was not so much the fear of bullet or bomb which put me off as the feeling of inadequacy. Nevertheless I asked God about it and two thoughts came to me.

a) Go and find out how to pray for the Irish people.
b) Go and repent for the sins of the English people.

I could certainly do that. I was also influenced by the very special person who asked me to go.

Eiblin Finn has been a Roman Catholic all her life although not a very committed one until recently. When her fifth child was born she suffered post-natal depression, went in and out of hospital much of the time, took strong anti-depressant tablets and felt very suicidal. Her family loved her but nothing registered. She simply wanted to leave the planet.

Eiblin was so desperate that she eventually allowed people to take her to a charismatic healing meeting. Everyone present was Catholic but that did not stop them from worshipping with hands in the air and banging tambourines. Eiblin thought she knew patients in her psychiatric ward who were more sane than this. Worship is not a spectator sport and until the Holy Spirit released Eiblin's own spirit to praise God it all looked very strange to her. At the end of the meeting the laying-on of hands was offered. Having tried everything else, Eiblin tried God. The priest asked her what she wanted. 'I want my little boy back,' she said simply. For three-and-a-half years Eiblin had been too ill to look after him herself. She closed her eyes, held out her hands, thought of Jesus and the priest prayed for her.

'Wonderful love came into my heart,' testifies Eiblin. 'It felt as though an iron bar came up from my ankles, through my knees and out of my head. "Jesus is alive," I thought. "He has healed me." '

Outside the grass was green and the birds were singing. Previously her silent world had appeared only in black and white. Having been buried for three years Eiblin suddenly rose from the dead and as she did God seemed to speak to her. 'Now that you have been healed I want you to concentrate on two things: 1) Bringing people of different denominations together. 2) Evangelism.'

Eiblin returned home with a big smile on her face. Her husband was waiting for her. 'I've met somebody I love more than you,' she said. 'You've been gone long enough,' he replied without raising an eyebrow. For some time he watched her carefully. She became very strange. Singing worship songs in the kitchen. Dancing with the ironing. Talking non-stop to Jesus. To her good Catholic hubby it didn't seem like a healing at all.

Eiblin's husband called in a local doctor. Without anyone seeing him come in he watched her strange antics from the doorway of the kitchen for some time. After some deliberation he pronounced her sane, but she continued to drive everyone else round the bend. She kept telling her friends about Jesus; nagged her husband to be born again and battered her poor parish priest with the idea of being baptised in the Holy Spirit. 'Lord,' he kept praying privately, 'why have you sent her to persecute me?'

Eventually the whole family came to a new and living relationship with Jesus. The priest accepted the change in the family as from God and supported the proposed visit to Ireland with prayer, publicity and petrol money. I accepted the invitation to join the group which was going to Ireland. It isn't easy to say 'no' to Eiblin and when God sides with her they form a dynamic duo!

A whole year was spent in prayer, fasting, instruction and preparation for the venture. Many Protestants and Catholics prayed for us and with us and came to the monthly public meetings. Some of us even attended lectures at Birmingham University on Irish history. Altogether eleven Christians agreed to go on our mission of reconciliation. We planned our last public meeting on Tuesday, 31 August 1993, prior to sailing from Holyhead the following day.

On the Saturday before we left there was overnight rioting in the Maze prison leaving ten prison officers and three inmates injured. The Ulster Volunteer Force then proceeded to make threats against prison officers.

On the Sunday morning we all worshipped in our own churches where the various congregations prayed for us, promised to continue doing so and wished us well.

At nine o'clock on Monday morning the Roman Catholic mother-of-four, Teresa de Mogolian Dowds, aged forty-eight, was shot dead at her North Belfast home in front of the children. The Ulster Freedom Fighters admitted responsibility but claimed her husband was the intended target.

The team assembled on the Tuesday evening at a church in Birmingham. It was quite a motley crew: one born-and-bred Roman Catholic; two who had converted to Roman Catholicism; two who had converted from

Roman Catholicism (one Anglican and one Pentecostal); one Church of Christ; three Anglicans; one vicar and Alan. (Alan goes where the action is and during our trip to Ireland was 'an Anglican'.)

People filled the church to pray for us and pledged to continue doing so while we were away. My friend Brian preached and afterwards a young girl came up to me and said she would like to become a Christian. We led her in a time of prayer and commitment to Jesus, asked God to fill her with his Spirit and then gave her one of my books. It was a good start.

At ten minutes to midnight Stewart's Supermarket in Derriaghy was wrecked and more than seventy homes were damaged by a 400lb IRA bomb.

On the Wednesday morning we gathered for breakfast. At twenty-five minutes past eight the Roman Catholic Jim Bell, aged forty-nine, was shot dead by the UVF outside an ice-cream factory in East Belfast.

The minibus arrived. Four and luggage in my car; seven, luggage and equipment in the small minibus, and picking up Eiblin's daughter on the way home. They had to be joking! Surely? And what equipment! Guitar, overhead projector, two collections of song-books and a box of assorted musical instruments.

We pushed and shoved, squeezed, repacked, breathed in and slammed the door shut. Unfortunately this left no room for oxygen and as the windows were opened the exhaust-pipe fell off! I suppose Eiblin's daughter will go in the box with the instruments on the way back, I thought to myself.

My suggestion that we went quickly to a garage to have a new exhaust-pipe fitted was instantly rejected. I sat reading the paper while they had a go with chewing-gum, blu-tak and string. We only had a copy of *The Sun* between us but someone kindly took page three out before handing it to the Vicar lest he be offended. I was glad people were praying for us. I read the paper through several times.

It was nearer to lunch-time than breakfast when we eventually set off for the afternoon boat from Holyhead. The sun shone all the way. I had been to Wales many times before, but had never previously seen the hills around Llangollen bathed in sunlight. It was glorious.

At half-past twelve two bombs containing 750lbs of explosives were found near Cullyhanna in South Armagh.

We didn't have time to stop for lunch but made do with whatever sandwiches, loaves and fishes had come with us. Throughout the 1,200 mile drive, whenever discomfort caused our own spirits to sag, the sight of our brothers and sisters folded neatly into the minibus ahead cheered us up enormously.

At five minutes to two a couple of Roman Catholic workers were injured in a Red Hand Commando murder attempt at York Crescent in North Belfast.

We caught the boat—just. The crossing was marvellous. We reclined luxuriously in spacious seats looking out on a calm sea beneath clear blue skies while inside the Irish fiddlers, whistlers, dancers and singers entertained us.

The minibus broke down in Dublin. I am not sure if we were beyond the Pale or not.[1] We pulled up outside a row of terraced houses and people rushed out to help us. 'What's the trouble?' they asked. 'No water,' Alan explained. Alan did all the explaining on our trip. Whenever the bus stopped and a door was opened, Alan fell out. No one else could move.

'To be sure that's no trouble at all—at all,' responded our Irish friends as jugs of water were brought out to us. When we thanked them for their help they used the phrases which followed us all over Ireland—North and South—'Yer very welcum!'

We drove North to the historic city of Drogheda with the Irish Sea on our right. Crossing the wide bridge over the River Boyne was a sombre moment. The setting sun gave it a blood-red appearance. This is where, in 1649, Cromwell began his campaign of revenge for the uprising of 1641. In some ways it was the last stage of the great Civil War: but the slaughter, for which Cromwell gave God all the glory, left no priest alive. Robert Kee writes: 'It has branded the name of the town into Irish history, as a traditionally classical example of English "frightfulness" in Ireland.'[2]

This was the river beside which the protestant King, William of Orange, defeated the Catholic James II in 1690; an event still celebrated today by Orange marches and commemorated as a bank holiday in the North. The remembering of this victory is often linked to the slogan which came into being as the besieged city of Derry held out successfully against James II—'No surrender'. In 1641, 59 per cent of Ireland's land was held by Catholics but by 1714 it was only 7 per cent. The loss of land by Catholics in Ireland is still known as the curse of Cromwell.

We were tired by the time we entered Northern Ireland. For someone like myself who has never seen war, it was very sobering to be stopped at a check-point by men in uniforms toting machine-guns. More friendly faces were waiting for us at the Renewal Centre in Rostrevor when we arrived. We were made 'very welcum' with food and hot drinks.[3]

At half past ten at night, prison officer Jim Peacock was shot dead by the UVF in the Oldpark area of North Belfast.

The beds of many Christian centres often feel as if they were thrown out by second-class hotels some twenty years ago but not this time. These were new, with enough room for a 6′2″ Vicar. The house was beautifully decorated and all the rooms spotlessly maintained. I'd recommend this place to any of my friends. We slept well that night.

At eleven o'clock that same night, prison officers' cars parked in the Rathcoole and Rathfern estates in Newtownabbey, north of Belfast, were set on fire by petrol bombs. At ten to twelve a prison officer, his wife and three children escaped injury when shots were fired through the bedroom window of their house at Mallusk Gardens in Antrim. At one o'clock another prison officer's car and garage were destroyed in a malicious blaze at Alexandra Park Avenue in North Belfast.

The good weather was still with us in the morning. From our bedroom windows we could see the serene Carlingford Lough with a gun-boat anchored in the middle of the water. Our rooms in the former mansion of the Earl of Kilmorey looked out on the Republic of Ireland, but behind us Ulster's Mountains of Mourne swept down to the sea. The Christian Renewal Centre is situated very much on the border.

It was a thrill to be welcomed by Cecil and Myrtle Kerr. They were very supportive. Earlier in the year some people had advised me not to go to Ireland. Do-gooders from England had not done much good in the past. 'Signs and wonders' people on a hit-and-run mission were likely to stir up more superstitions in a land already full of too many leprechauns.

I was helped to overcome these fears on renewing acquaintance with David Gillett at an Anglican Renewal Ministry's conference in Derbyshire at the start of the year. David had spent some time with Cecil and Myrtle at Rostrevor and written a most helpful book on reconciliation and renewal in Northern Ireland. He encouraged me to go. I went home and reread David's book in which he wrote this:

> We, the English, are the ones who should take the lead. I say this for several reasons. First, because I am English, and we should remove first the beam from our own eye.... Secondly, because history shows in the

> very broadest terms, 'We started it.' Thirdly, because it is easier for *us*.... We repent, of course, not only to release the injured party, but also because *we* are guilty and *we* need to be forgiven.[4]

I found this challenging. I also found a biblical base for doing this in the book of Daniel. The prophet is in exile in Babylon with many others from Judah. After reading the prophecy of Jeremiah, he 'turned to the Lord God and pleaded with him in prayer and petition, in fasting, and in sackcloth and ashes.' Some of the words he uses spoke particularly to me:

> We have sinned and done wrong. We have been wicked and have rebelled; we have turned away from your commands and laws.... We have sinned against you. The Lord our God is merciful and forgiving, even though we have rebelled against him; we have not obeyed the Lord our God or kept the laws he gave us through his servants the prophets. All Israel has transgressed your law and turned away, refusing to obey you.
>
> Therefore the curses and sworn judgments written in the Law of Moses, the servant of God, have been poured out on us, because we have sinned against you (Dan 9:5,8–11).

The response is powerful.

> While I was speaking and praying, confessing my sin and the sin of my people Israel and making my request to the Lord my God for his holy will—while I was still in prayer, Gabriel...came to me in swift flight (Dan 9:20–21).

The battle is then fought in the heavenlies. Another mighty angel and Michael, the Archangel, fight against the prince of the Persian kingdom and in due course the people of Judah are set free and allowed to return to their own land. Presumably this is the biblical basis for some of Piretti's exciting novels, but I could not help noticing that it is *repentance* and prayer—not just prayer—which leads to victory.[5]

Daniel was a good man. It is not his sin which cursed the people, but nevertheless he repented of it on their behalf. To confess is to see sin the same way as God sees it. Daniel did not make excuses for his people, he confessed their sin. To repent is to turn from sin, not to repeat it. Orange marches celebrate and often repeat the sins of long ago. We in England sometimes think this is absurd, especially as it happened in 1690, yet every fifth of November we burn effigies of a Roman Catholic Guy who tried to stop James I from oppressing Catholics—and that goes back to 1605!

To repent is to turn from it as Daniel had all his life. To renounce it is to declare to the world that sin is sin and we stand against it, even if it means being fed to the lions. I believe if we confess, repent and renounce the sins of our ancestors, not only will we and those who have been sinned against be affected, but so will satanic strongholds in the heavenlies. I think Ireland could do with a bit of help from Gabriel and Michael.

Cecil and Myrtle were delighted that we came and they spent quality time praying with us and for us. Cecil shared how he'd spent many hours in his youth arguing and debating, preaching and theologising with those of a different persuasion only to find the barriers became higher and the people more entrenched. 'When the Spirit of reconciliation is released through the cross of Christ,' he said, 'then barriers are broken down and Christians come together in love and fellowship.'

That night we saw it in action. Protestants and Catholics prayed with one another in the lounge for the bereaved, the injured and those who had pulled the triggers. It was a very moving moment for all of us. Jim Burke, an Irish American Catholic priest, joined us for prayer prior to his own interdenominational Mission of Hope undertaken in the province with Cecil. He too was very kind and full of enthusiasm for our trip.

That night more bombs went off in Armagh but no one was hurt.

The following day we left Rostrevor and drove to a house half way between Kiltimagh and Swinford, County Mayo. This was the venue of the first meeting at which I was due to speak. Road-blocks, uniforms, machine-guns, barbed wire and armoured vehicles greeted us as we entered Armagh, the ecclesiastical capital of Ireland. This is the seat of both the Protestant and the Catholic Archbishops.

From the by-pass we could see how the small town of about 13,000 people was totally dominated by the two cathedrals standing on the hill. The twin-spired Catholic building was finished in 1873 and the Church of Ireland one with its battlemented central tower was extensively restored in 1837. Both are dedicated to St Patrick—at least one do-gooder who came over and did good.

We stopped for lunch at Enniskillen where Cecil Kerr grew up as a boy. He knew several of the eleven who were killed by a bomb at the Remembrance Sunday service on 8 November, 1987. Sometimes when he speaks at big meetings Stephen Ross accompanies him and gives his testimony. Stephen became a Christian a short while before being present where the bomb exploded. He was critically ill for weeks but survived to declare his forgiveness for the killers.

We drove past the memorial to the eleven which stands at the entrance of the town. Who could forget the story of Gordon Wilson holding hands with his daughter while buried under the rubble? 'Daddy, I love you very much,' she said and died. Gordon, like Stephen, found the needed grace to forgive the killers.

As we left the city we passed the police station. The high walls, look-out post, reinforced metal doors and barbed wire reminded us all of pictures we had seen of prisoner-of-war camps. Shortly afterwards we left Ulster for Connaught and the journey became a comedy of errors.

An accident blocked the main road; we turned round and became hopelessly lost; the minibus broke down; we prayed and a cow appeared from behind a hedge; we prayed again and Alan was attacked by an Alsatian from a nearby house; the rest of us escaped into the vehicles; we prayed again and the bus rattled on slowly 'mit sparken und bangen'; we met a South African Christian and gave him a signed book; we've still got his pen; we arrived at the home near Kiltimagh for our first meeting with five minutes to spare and no time for dinner.

Friends of Eiblin crowded into the lounge and spilled over into the kitchen—a large lavish kitchen. We began to question the postcards we had seen of small quaint Irish cottages. Were they just for the tourists? Most of the homes we visited were large and luxurious.

Geoff and Eiblin shared brief testimonies. Geoff had married an Irish girl, attended lessons and lectures on Roman Catholicism, but refused to convert until God told him to do so. Doreen shared how Eiblin and the charismatic Catholics of Ireland had helped her to overcome childhood problems created by an RC education in Jamaica.

Then I was on. I was introduced as a priest in the Church of England. I began by confessing and repenting of some English sins which I believed had been committed against the Irish. They were all taken completely by surprise at this and didn't quite know how to respond but the atmosphere definitely softened and became more open. After a short address the Holy Spirit came powerfully on most of those who were present.

A number seemed to be almost 'out' in the Spirit—

standing up. There wasn't any room to lie down. Some managed to find seats. One lady squeezed Beth's hand when she came round and said 'thanks'. Her beaming peaceful face said it all. Others were not so fortunate. In the confined space it was not always easy to stop those unfamiliar with this ministry from interrupting what God was doing.

I gave a 'word' for someone who'd had a hard life and others recognised a lady whom it fitted. The Lord was beginning to move powerfully on her as she lay sprawled across an armchair when a sharp elbow dug her in the ribs and a voice said, 'Come on now, sleeping beauty, wake up!' She continued to elbow her until the lady came round with a bump, looked startled, felt guilty for having been 'out' and receiving a blessing, and went to make the tea.

Little Bridie was also enjoying the Lord, flat out on the sofa, when a hand appeared from behind it. Suddenly the hand grabbed a chunk of her hair and scalp, shook it vigorously, and was accompanied by the cry of: 'Wake up, Bridie. To be sure you'll be missing the tea.' Fortunately Kay managed to rescue the situation and recommence ministry. Bridie had also suffered from a hard life and used to have a drink problem, which the Lord was now helping her to control. God really affirmed her and in the end Bridie confessed to feeling very peaceful and loved.

The Lord delivered a lady from a spirit of anxiety and I met with someone who was claiming a 'word' I had given. It concerned serious bereavement problems: the lady in question had lost two grown-up children through separate road accidents and a third member of the family in tragic circumstances. Wherever we went we seemed to come across premature deaths through non-terrorist means: accidents, disease, still births and miscarriages. There seemed to be a curse of 'death' in many of the places we visited. We prayed, affirmed and did what we could. The Lord came powerfully on many such people.

The following day we visited Eiblin's aunties—two saintly, elderly prayer warriors who said they prayed for me and a number of other priests regularly. They lived miles from anywhere in an old whitewashed stone house, just like the ones on the postcards, with no running water, no proper heating and no flushing toilet. Until recently they had used the barn where the cows were kept. Following a visit to the aunties one person was overheard in the bathroom where she was staying saying, 'Thank you Lord for running water. Thank you Lord for flushing toilets'—accompanied by suitable sound effects. I am delighted to say that the finest of modern amenities were available to us wherever we stayed.

We had been informally invited to Knock twelve months previously but due to a communications problem the written invitation was only received two weeks before departure date. Despite this the Mission organisers were convinced the Lord was bringing the team to Knock and continued to pray and fast for this venue. We found the charismatic Father Joe, who had invited us to Knock, hugged and prayed together and were back on schedule.

Interesting things happened during the afternoon before the evening meeting. Eiblin took some of us into Kiltimagh to meet the priest but we failed to find him. An assistant priest had just moved in so Eiblin took us there. A young priest called Adrian answered the door, invited us in and after introductions announced he'd been reading one of my books in the confessional the day before. Eiblin had met him on one of her previous visits to Ireland and given him the book, but no one knew he'd moved to Kiltimagh.

Angela, Doreen, Pat and Margaret went for a meal in a restaurant at Knock. After tucking into egg and chips a man in his thirties at the next table opened up a conversation with them.

'Are you staying in Knock?' he began.

'No. We're staying in Swinford a few miles away,' they replied.

'Are you on holiday in Ireland?' he asked rather more hesitantly. There was a short difficult pause before Angela felt prompted to reply.

'No,' she said, 'We're a group of eleven Christians of mixed denominations, Catholics and Protestants, and we're on a mission of reconciliation to Ireland.'

'I thought you were something like that,' he responded. 'I was listening to your conversation. Do you believe miracles happen here?' he continued. Angela replied cautiously.

'I don't know,' she began. 'All I know is that when you pray in the name of Jesus and ask the Holy Spirit to come miracles do sometimes happen.' He pondered over this but readily joined them when invited.

The man was travelling from Northern Ireland to the far South on business. In his own words he recounted how he'd recently become a Christian, left the Catholic church and now worshipped with his wife in a Methodist church, but was quite angry about Roman Catholicism.

Angela spoke to him about truth and grace, explaining how truth without grace could have a hard edge and alienate people, while grace without truth can send us off in many directions creating a god in our own image. They offered to pray for him and he readily agreed.

At the laying-on-of-hands in the restaurant the man began to cry. The Holy Spirit deeply convicted him and started to melt his heart. The encounter only lasted twenty minutes, but this was why we had come. Those who witnessed it felt that even if nothing else happened during the trip, this meeting made both the visit and the discomfort in the minibus worth while.

There were about two hundred people assembled in the Blessed Sacrament Chapel at Knock when I stood up to speak. A number came from the surrounding prayer groups; a few priests attended; at least one nun and many who were on pilgrimage to Knock came in to see what was happening. I confessed and repented of the sins of the English people as I saw them, mentioning the plantation policy of James I, Oliver Cromwell, William of Orange and the potato famine. As soon as I had done this an Irish lady leapt to her feet and confessed the sins of the Irish people to the English. There seemed to be a murmur of agreement before we said the 'Our Father' together—'forgive us our sins as we forgive those who sin against us!'

It was very good to hear this. I had been concentrating on the sins of the English because I felt God wanted me to repent for our part in the bad feelings and wars. This reminded me that in any conflict there is always two sides and sins which need to be confessed by both parties.

After 'a few old stories and jokes' as Alan put it, we invited the Holy Spirit to come among us. They were very open and many were greatly blessed. One man had been in Knock for the day and came to the meeting thinking it was a mass. As he was filled with the Holy Spirit his face radiated the presence of Christ. A lady visiting from Canada swayed from side to side continually and asked excitedly afterwards if it was always like this.

A more local person asked for prayer about a leg problem but was soon pouring out her heart to one of our team: a husband drowned as a young man; a son now an alcoholic; and her own loneliness. The team member sensed the need for listening not only to the person but to God. It was as she shared accurate 'words' about the situation that God took them deeper and deeper into the problem.

There was a nun from the local community who'd met Cecil Kerr many times and was very much into renewal and reconciliation. She was sorry she couldn't stay for ministry, but was rushing to get back 'in' to the convent otherwise she would be 'out' for the night. A young man from Dublin, just passing through, came to the service, was amazed by what he heard, saw and experienced for himself. He said he had been touched by God and had never felt anything like it before. He went away beaming, armed with books.

The lady who had been elbowed out of a blessing the night before came and received uninterrupted comfort and joy from the Lord. She had not only lost her own husband but killed a child herself in a road accident. It was not her fault, but one of our team was able to minister by God's grace into the guilt and false guilt. Premature death seemed to be among the people wherever we went in this land full of sadness and heartache.

After the meeting Father Joe approached me with his Bible in one hand. He asked me what I thought about a particular passage. This seemed a little odd as I could find nothing in it related to anything I had been saying—and then I twigged. This was the lectionary passage for Sunday morning; it was gone midnight and he hadn't yet prepared a sermon. There, at the front of the church, we laughed together, opened our Bibles and shared a few thoughts.

This was the abiding memory that members of our party took away with them. Catholic and Protestant priests laughing together, sharing thoughts on God's word, Bibles in hand, visible for all to see. There will be no religion in heaven because God himself will be there. We shall see him as he really is and together we will worship him.

'I did not see a temple in the city, because the Lord God Almighty and the Lamb are its temple' (Rev 21:22). John also saw in his vision the end of national pride, divisions and war. 'And the leaves of the tree are for the healing of the nations' (Rev 22:2).

Endnotes

1. In the reign of Henry II much land was taken from the native inhabitants and given to the English settlers. There grew up side by side two distinct classes, one dominant and landowning, the other servile and landless. The English lived within the district around Dublin called the Pale, and referred to the 'lower classes' who lived elsewhere as 'beyond the Pale'. When I checked my history and consulted the maps afterwards I realised we were clearly within the Pale and not beyond it when we stopped for water.
2. Robert Kee, *Ireland A History The book of the major BBC Television Series* (Weidenfield and Nicholson Ltd.: London, 1980).
3. The Christian Renewal Centre was established in 1974 to be a place of prayer, renewal and reconciliation. Anyone wishing to visit it should write to: The Christian Renewal Centre, Shore Road, Rostrevor, Newry, Co. Down BT34 3ET, Northern Ireland.
4. David Gillett, *The Darkness Where God Is* (Kingsway Publications: Eastbourne, 1983), p 135.
5. Frank Peretti, *This Present Darkness* (Minstrel: Eastbourne, 1989). Frank Peretti, *Piercing the Darkness* (Minstrel: Eastbourne, 1990).

CHAPTER

7

The Healing of the Nations

Our visit to Knock was not an easy one for most of us. On 21 August, 1879, several people from the village claimed to see an apparition outside the church. It consisted of Joseph, Mary and John the evangelist carrying an open book; an altar with a lamb on it, a cross behind and angels hovering above. The apparition lasted about two hours. The witnesses said the bright light which illuminated the whole scene was at its most intense on the lamb in the centre.

I have no problem with this vision. John holding the book of Revelation, the Lamb who was slain and the angels worshipping. This is God's word. It is a picture which many Christians find helpful as they worship the Lord. I have no problem with seeing Joseph and Mary in this same picture particularly as Mary is seen pointing to the lamb.

My problem is that for many Knock has become a Marian shrine. The largest building on the site is known as the Basilica of Our Lady, Queen of Ireland, which was officially inaugurated as such by Pope John Paul II. According to one of the official booklets people come to give 'intense devotion to Our Lady at her Shrine in Knock'. Every shop in the High Street and stall in the market place sells statues of Mary. The Protestant in me felt somewhat uncomfortable at this preoccupation with just one member of the early church (Acts 1: 14).[1]

On the other hand my Catholic friends have told me that the preaching of God's word and the blessing of the sick in Jesus' name during which healings take place are big attractions at Knock for most people. It is also becoming a favoured place for reconciliation, confession and the Eucharist as Mary in the representations of the apparition points to the Lamb who takes away our sins. Every part of Knock which points people to Jesus has my approval.

The foundation stone on which Roman Catholicism rests is Jesus Christ. I do not agree with some of the building but I do believe in the cornerstone. This is why I consider believing Roman Catholics to be brothers and sisters in Christ.

When I was in Rostrevor I picked up a leaflet entitled 'What is an Evangelical Catholic?' It makes interesting reading. A number of well-known Roman Catholic leaders have given their names to it. Here are some of the things that it states:

> Evangelical Catholics would affirm:
>
> That salvation cannot be earned—it is a free gift. However, the evidence of good deeds indicating that one has become a committed Christian must then follow.
>
> That there is only one mediator between God and men, the person of Jesus Christ (1 Tim 2:5).
>
> The priesthood of all believers which means that a Christian has direct access to the Father through Jesus.
>
> That Scripture in its entirety (both Old and New Testaments) is the inspired, authoritative word of God.
>
> That the Eucharist (or Mass) is not a repetition of Calvary, ie, Jesus died once for all. The priest and

people enter into that one all-sufficient sacrifice by grace.

Heaven for those who accept the salvation won by Jesus and hell for those who die unrepentant for their wickedness.

That all human beings are born into a state of separation from God as a result of the fall.

That Jesus died on the cross in atonement for all sin, and that in his death he took the place of all sinners in bearing their guilt (Is 53:6).

That Jesus will come again in glory to judge the living and the dead.

Evangelical Catholics would believe that:

1) The Roman Catholic Church is a Christian church that has taken on some un-Christian practices over the centuries. However, a major renewal of the Holy Spirit has and is taking place directly as a result of the Second Vatican Council addressing some of these issues.

2) The Holy Spirit is moving to bring both renewal and revival in the Roman Catholic Church as in other Christian churches.

3) Many members of the Roman Catholic Church, while being perhaps over-sacramentalised have been under-evangelised and therefore its members need to be challenged as adults to accept Jesus as personal Lord and Saviour. In the words of Pope Paul VI in his Encyclical on Evangelisation—'The Church exists in order to evangelise.... She begins by first being evangelised herself.'

Evangelical Catholics are committed to:

Jesus as the only way to salvation—one day every knee shall bow and every tongue confess that Jesus Christ is truly Lord.

The necessity of the empowering of the Holy Spirit

for the committed Christian to achieve his/her full potential and do the works of Christ.

The priority of evangelism within the life of the local Catholic Church as well as a commitment to join with committed Christians in other denominations in the fulfilment of the biblical command to take Christ to all the nations.[2]

I too would affirm, believe and am committed to these Christian truths. This is why I was happy to teach and minister in the name of Jesus at the invitation of those with similar beliefs. This is why I am happy to be remembered standing beside Father Joe, Bibles in hand, sharing God's truth with one another, in a chapel at Knock.

On the Sunday morning we planned our own reconciliation meeting followed by the breaking of bread together. Some of our party had been left behind the previous day and missed lunch. Others had been very annoyed at my watching cricket on the television for an hour and a half just before the big meeting at Knock. The ladies didn't seem to register the importance of the Nat.West. Cricket final at Lords in which Warwickshire were taking part. Neither were they impressed when I told them that our team from Birmingham had won, making a record score in the second innings. We needed to sort a few things out.

First, our party of eleven apologised to one another accompanied with hugs and then I explained the theology of cricket. It is common in evangelical circles to gather together half-an-hour before a big meeting and pray like mad. If people do not join in such activity they are always considered unspiritual or not caring enough about the meeting. A lecture on the importance of prayer will then be delivered.

But some time ago I began to notice that those who move most powerfully in things of the Holy Spirit do not normally pray just before a big meeting. I asked one of them why. 'The time just before a big meeting,' he explained to me, 'is not the time to pray. It is the time to trust.' I knew instantly what he meant.

If I ask someone to bring an overhead projector to a meeting at 5 pm and ring him up at 4.30 pm to remind him, am I expressing trust or fear? Those who have really learnt to trust Jesus will often pray all day and every day of the week preceding a meeting, but may play on the computer an hour before it is due to begin. It says to God, Satan and myself, my trust is in Jesus Christ and not my ability to remind him of things just before kick-off. It is always good to pray but there are some occasions when the exercising of faith is as important as asking for it.

We shared communion together. It needed to be very sensitively handled. I explained to them I was not wearing my clerical collar and we would not be using any liturgy. It was not a Roman Catholic Mass nor a Church of England Eucharist. It would be a few friends worshipping, praying, reading the Bible, eating bread and drinking wine together. The passage we read was 1 Corinthians 11:23–26. It proved to be very meaningful and deeply moving for all those who took part.

Fitted with a new fuel-filter, the minibus roared off the next day in the direction of Galway City. We were hoping to see the sun go down over the bay.[3] We sang a song or said a poem for every place we visited. We followed sedately behind the metal and flesh sandwich and were soon on our own. They left us behind. We pressed on regardless. In due course the inhabitants of the little bus discovered our absence and turned round to look for us. It was very kind of them, but unfortunately they failed. I'd eaten a meal, soaked in the bath and was fast asleep in bed by the time the leaders of our party arrived.

The meeting in Galway was organised by a Franciscan priest in a brown habit and matching sandals. He'd heard about the meeting in Knock and was pleased to 'welcum' us.

This was the first of three meetings taking place in people's homes at which over a hundred people were present. The owners had knocked out some of the inner walls several years ago in order to accomodate the crowds attending the prayer meetings. I sat by the priest and his accordion in a small alcove as the various adjoining rooms began to fill up with young people. I felt reasonably secure until someone arrived with drums and began assembling them next to me. The worship was loud and joyful.

Some of our own team received ministry during the day, including deliverance, and were prepared for what the Lord wanted to do that night. Beth wrote this down for me:

> When Peter gave his talk and then called on the Holy Spirit to come, it was no surprise to me that God came in such power. I don't know if anything could have surprised me that evening. I was resting totally in God's love and I wished it would never end.
>
> I turned round to minister to a young girl who was standing behind me and was obviously engaged mightily in the Spirit. There was no way she could have fallen down, there just wasn't room but, yet again, she was out! The girl was wearing glasses and the lights were quite dim so when I first saw her one eye open slowly I thought I might have imagined it.
>
> As I stood facing her with my hand on her head, her left eye opened slowly again and looked directly at me. I was certainly not imagining it this time. I felt a chill, as if the room had gone cold. Peter was still giving out words of knowledge at this point and there was no sound in the room except for the occasional sobbing. 'Oh,' I thought. 'I think I've got one!'
>
> I looked at the girl again and as the one eye opened I started to speak in tongues. It didn't like that and neither did it like the mention of the blood of Jesus

even though this was all done under my breath. Very quietly I commanded it by the blood of Jesus to leave. Both eyes opened wide and filled the whole of her eye sockets. I couldn't see the glasses any more. All I could see were these glaring eyes and I knew its name was 'Anger'.

The chill was there again. When I commanded 'Anger' to leave in the name of Jesus she blinked a few times, the eyes returned to normality and the chill had gone.

The young girl testified afterwards that she had never felt the presence of the Holy Spirit so powerfully before. At first she felt afraid, but now she felt 'lovely'. She wanted the gift of tongues, but didn't feel worthy of such a gift. How often we met this feeling of unworthiness! Some ladies took her into a side room for more prayer.

Ann helped a young girl to understand that there is no condemnation in Christ Jesus. Even though she had been to a priest for confession, she thought she was so very wicked and was never going to heaven as the Lord would never forgive her. Ann answered her otherwise from Scripture.

Kay ministered to another young girl who responded to a 'word' about a particular sin. When she realised God's forgiveness could make her whole again she cried and cried.

Margaret and Alan felt led to ask one young man who was glued to his seat to stand so they could pray for him. Angela joined in, laid a hand gently on his head, and over he went. As people ministered to him on the floor he sensed God giving him a special anointing. He was soon to become a priest.

While the team were ministering to several individuals, the Franciscan priest asked my advice about all kinds of spiritual matters and bought a number of our books. He asked us to lay on hands and minister to him which we did.

Kay and Beth met another lady who wanted to speak in tongues. 'Step this way,' they said and led her to the appropriate room. There she found her daughter, the one who'd received some deliverance, resting in the Spirit and singing in tongues. As they prayed over her mother she too burst into tongues for the first time. After the ministry was concluded they asked Ann and Angela when they could feel this good again and were advised to stay close to Jesus all the time.

On the following morning we prayed for a man in a wheelchair. He was suffering from Motor Neurone Disease, and was accompanied by his wife, Moira. This was another very sad situation. She had lost two children and now seemed likely to lose her husband. We prayed our best prayers and God did seem to touch them both. Following this time of ministry Moira became pregnant again.

Some time afterwards, when he became ill with a chest infection, Moira struggled spiritually until they said the Lord's prayer together. As they did so she was able to release him and came into a spiritual freedom herself. Moira said she had never felt so completely free and there was a great peace between the two of them as he died.

We continue to pray for this particular family who, despite their circumstances, are still going on with the Lord. They are a lesson and example to many of us. The Irish seem to know a lot about suffering.

In the afternoon we drove to Rathkeale near Limerick via Bunratty Castle. Irish tea towels and postcards show many beautiful castles, pubs and cottages, but I found the churches to be the most interesting. Every big village or small town we drove through had a cathedral-sized church dominating its high street.

If there are a thousand people living in a place they need a church which seats a thousand people because everyone attends. It is not quite the same in the inner-cities but in the towns and villages it makes the building dominant and the priest very powerful. This is why religion is such an important issue. It involves everyone. In England, where only ten per cent of the people attend church, and most of our relatively small churches are more than half empty, religion is a minority issue and the clergy are sidelined. It certainly felt different speaking and ministering in a religious country rather than in the secular society to which I am accustomed.

The meeting that evening in Ashkeaton, near Rathkeale, was held in a greenhouse—a hundred-seater sun lounge built onto the back of the house. This was the one and only appearance of our overhead projector. They had two of their own but having brought ours we decided to use it. I sat on the very front row next to Beth. When the first song appeared on the screen neither of us could read a word because the letters were so small.

'Hey Beth,' I said. 'Did they bring a box of binoculars as well?' I'm afraid we rather giggled through the first couple of worship songs but I think God understood. He seemed to be with us. As usual I didn't get on to speak in the glass-roofed extension until after 10 pm, but ministry went on throughout half the night.

In my talk I explained that we don't become Christians by going to church any more than we become tomatoes by entering a greenhouse! They smiled. The sun lounge was full when I asked the Holy Spirit to come and so were several other rooms in the house. People swayed alternately about 45° giving the appearance of moving piano keys. This was an evening of blessing. Many faces looked very peaceful, out in the Spirit, unable to fall due to lack of space, but gently swaying in the breeze.

Alan ministered to one smartly-dressed man whose hands were moving back and forth as if he was playing the piano. He shared afterwards how he was led during this time to think of a friend who'd suffered from shoulder pain for many years. In his mind he'd been smoothing his friend's shoulders with his hands and when Alan laid hands on him he felt great power coming into his hands.

After the meeting I met a man who showed me his tattered Bible. Two years ago he'd been known as the local drunk, often found lying in the gutter at the side of the road. This group had helped him to receive Jesus as his Lord and Saviour and since then he'd not had another drink. Instead he now spends hours a day reading his Bible.

We were presented with a fifty-six-pound bag of potatoes to take home with us. As a symbolic gesture of reconciliation following the potato famine of the last century we could hardly refuse. It looked good in the minibus. Judging from the hospitality we received and my observations of their habits I have now come to this conclusion: the Irish eat twice as much as we do and this means they don't have to sleep.

It is not far from Rathkeale to the mouth of the Shannon. Here the golf-courses of Ballybunion look down on the rollers of the Atlantic Ocean beyond which lies the North American coast. It is a pity they could not find room for my clubs in the minibus.

We drove on to Tralee, paused for a song and then tackled the Dingle peninsula. It was here that they filmed *Ryan's Daughter*. It is here that they boast the most westerly golf-course in Europe. It was here that I found myself captivated by the atmosphere. This was Ireland as I always imagined it to be. Misty drizzle soaking the Slieve Mish Mountains, surrounded by Atlantic breakers on both sides. The sun broke through as we headed towards the vast beach at Inch, giving a shimmering effect to the water of Castlemaine Harbour which lay beyond.

I wanted to stay. I could imagine myself in a little cottage tucked into the side of the hills looking out to Inch Point, being overcome with the desire to write and write. Undisturbed; uncluttered; a sense of mystery in the mist and awesome power in the waves. This was the land of Joyce, Yeats, and the birthplace of C.S. Lewis and I wanted to be a part of it.

There seems to be something literary and artistic about the West—like San Francisco and Vancouver on the other side of the pond. Eiblin and Ann danced a jig between the tables of a pub in Tralee amid much hilarity and then we moved on eastwards:—Tipperary—ate lunch, sang the song—bought the T-shirt—drove through Kilkenny—past its river, castle and cathedral—and on to the frontier town of Carlow for our final meeting.

Our hosts greeted us like all the others. As they flung their arms around us the automatic but sincerely meant liturgical phrase was uttered for the last time—'Yer very welcum.' And then we were sat down, mug in hand, for a serious history lesson.

On 24 April, 1916, the Dublin General Post Office became the headquarters of the Easter Rising. 300 civilians, 60 rebels and 130 British troops were killed before they surrendered on 29 April. A few days after the surrender it was announced that three of the leaders had been shot. If the executions had stopped there, future history might have been different. But they continued for ten days, adding another thirteen to the number.

W.B. Yeats expressed in poetry the problems which then arose.

> O but we talked at large before
> The sixteen men were shot,
> But who can talk of give and take,
> What should be and what not
> While those dead men are loitering there
> To stir the boiling pot?[4]

In 1919 the Irish Volunteers were reconstituted as the Irish Republican Army. In 1920 partition of the island was set up with independent parliaments for North and South by the Government of Ireland Act. In 1921 the first parliament of Northern Ireland was opened in Belfast by George V and in the South the Irish Free State was established. All this led to civil war and armed conflict between the Nationalists who accepted partition and those who opposed it.

The British government during this time was very short of troops as a result of the First World War. Consequently they decided to take convicts out of prisons and use mercenaries who came for the money. They kitted them out as best they could with uniforms and weapons and sent them to Ireland. Many of them had Royal Navy tops with Army khaki bottoms. As they were first seen in County Tipperary they received a nickname after a famous pack of hounds there called the 'Black and Tans'. One of the garrison towns for this group of recruits was Carlow.

The IRA used guerrilla tactics, living anonymously among the Irish people most of the time. As a result of this the untrained thugs felt justified in committing atrocities against the ordinary people, many of whom were innocent, claiming they were harbouring rebels. Their cruelty with guns and bayonets are legendary in Carlow. Many of those who would be at the meeting had relatives and ancestors who'd suffered much at the hands of the Black and Tans—including murder.

A couple of years before we arrived, a building in Carlow was being demolished. For no apparent reason many young men in the area committed suicide. People from various prayer groups heard about this and on investigation discovered that this was a building where people had been hanged, some of whom had cursed the place prior to execution. The groups came together, prayed and broke the curses, and subsequently there were no more suicides.

One group also had some success in praying against

Coeliac disease. This is an intolerance to grain which can cause serious accumulative physical damage. Apparently, during the Irish Famine, the British paid informers and potential 'converts' with grain which some families accepted merely to keep their children alive. Unfortunately some who were angered by this put a curse on the grain. When this curse was broken in Jesus' name people in the area suffering from Coeliac disease were healed.

In the garden of our host's home was a meeting room which could hold one hundred and fifty people. They'd built it themselves. It was full when Geoff and Eiblin stood up to give their testimonies. After they finished I stood up, wearing my clerical collar, and publicly confessed, repented and renounced the sins of the English against the Irish, this time including the Black and Tans. By the time I invited the Holy Spirit to come on the gathered assembly there was an atmosphere of acceptance.

Ripples of mirth began breaking out almost immediately and then turned into great guffaws as the Holy Spirit removed tension and released joy in people all round the hall. We were told afterwards that the man who was laughing the loudest had suffered a series of tragedies in his life. Many were overjoyed to hear him laugh in the Spirit, not believing they would ever see him smile again.

When the time of ministry came to an end, I hoped to slip away and have some sleep before catching the early boat home. No chance. Our host encouraged people to share. Some stood up and asked to be forgiven for helping the IRA in the past and for sympathising with them. One lady realised she had been hating someone who killed her daughter in a car accident and asked to be forgiven and released from hatred. Forgiveness was a common theme.

Eventually a 'word' was given by a local person suggesting that everyone stood up and apologised to the English for the sins of the Irish. This was seen as a necessary step towards peace. Nearly everyone stood up and did as suggested.

One lady shared afterwards that she was initially unable to stand and do this, especially as it involved forgiving the British for the atrocities caused by the Black and Tans. Her grandmother's home had been burnt to the ground and her mother had found the dead body of grandmother by the side of the road. She wanted to stand but some force seemed to hold her back. Suddenly one of the team appeared acting on a 'word' from God and cut her off in the name of Jesus from all generational curses. Immediately she stood and, with tears in her eyes, gladly forgave us our sins.

The meeting was closed by an elderly priest. Aged seventy-two he was going to Nigeria the following day as a missionary, and had naturally retired to bed early. Suddenly the Lord woke him and told him to get up and come to our meeting. 'I never thought before,' he began, 'that we had to repent of our sins towards the English. Now I see it,' he said. He pronounced the final blessing on our little tour. As I hugged him afterwards several people wept.

We said goodbye to the minibus at Pembroke Dock, choosing to relax by the sea for a while. As it drove away into the distance it resembled a Giles' Cartoon. The large sack of potatoes and Eiblin's daughter were wedged in among the musical instruments, once-used OHP, boxes of never-used song-books, newly-acquired presents for home, luggage and bodies of various denominational shapes and sizes. God used them. Bless them. We drove home in comfort.

Some have criticised me for going with Catholics to Ireland and ministering to Catholics. They believe that the only way forward for Ireland is for many to leave the Roman Catholic Church, be saved and baptised in the Holy Spirit. I agree with the last two but not always with the first. It may, at times, be right for some, but it seems to me that Protestants have been trying to bring Catholics out since Henry VIII and it very definitely has not worked. Those who do not learn from history repeat it, and if ever there was a country which kept repeating its history it is Ireland.

I believe instead that we should all confess, repent and renounce the sins of our own history that we may be free from the Satanic curses which come from unforgiveness. It is only the Holy Spirit through the cross of Christ who can help us to do this.

Having said that, however, I do understand the problem. Droves of born-again charismatics have left the Church of England for the fresher pastures of house churches. Some could stand it no longer while others were asked to leave. I see the temptation for charismatic Catholics to do something similar in Ireland. It saddened me greatly to see meeting rooms built in private houses for charismatic meetings, rather than being held in the church with the blessing of the priest. If the Holy Spirit is not welcomed inside the structures, he will continue blowing wherever he wills even if it is outside the sanctuary, as John Wesley discovered many years ago.

How then shall we pray? For those who work for reconciliation and seek unity through renewal, like Cecil and Myrtle in Rostrevor; for priests such as Adrian in Kiltimagh and Joe who welcomed us to Knock; for Catholic charismatic leaders throughout the land as represented by the Galway Franciscan who opened doors for us and the young man soon to be ordained who went over in the power of the Holy Spirit; for the witness of reformed alcoholics such as those we met at Kiltimagh and Rathkeale and priests open to know more of God like the ones who attended the meeting in Carlow; for those who lead the Spirit-filled meetings we found dotted about the country; for the coming of the Holy Spirit in power, love and peace bringing more of the kingdom of God on earth as it is in heaven—a place where there is no religion but a healing of the nations; where there is no evil, sickness or any kind of death, and where the angels and saints gather around the throne to worship the lamb who was slain, for ever and ever. These, I believe, are the signs of God's kingdom which we can begin to taste 'on earth as in heaven' when we allow Jesus to fill us again and again with his Holy Spirit.

Endnotes

1. The quote comes from Fr. Michael Walsh, *The Glory of Knock* (Custodians of the Knock Shrine, 1958), p 19. It describes in particular the Marian Year of 1954 but has been appropriate for some since then.
2. The leaflet *What is an Evangelical Catholic* was published by forty-four well-known Roman Catholic leaders in June 1992. It is available from Evangelical Catholic Document, c/o 72 Hillcourt Road, Glenageary, Co. Dublin, Ireland.
3. We were surprised how many songs we knew from Irish places we visited. 'The Mountains of Mourne sweep down to the sea', 'Galway Bay', 'The Rose of Tralee', and 'It's a long way to Tipperary'. We also discovered many known 'Limericks' among us. A land of song and the arts.
4. W.B. Yeats, Sixteen Dead Men (1916). I took a verse of this poem from Benedict Kiely, *Yeats' Ireland, an Illustrated Anthology* (Aurum Press: London, 1989), p 96.

CHAPTER

8

What If I Am Not Healed?

Mary became a Christian when she was twenty-one. Having been around church and other Christians all her life it was a very definite commitment and she knew exactly what she was doing. Life became a lot of fun. Mary enjoyed Jesus and church and the security they gave her, and her enthusiasm for living led many people to become her friends.

Thoughts and hopes of marriage were never far away but Mary never let them dominate her, and now looks back with happy memories on her twenties. Working with young people and helping them to know Jesus is something she has always done well.

When Mary was twenty-eight she suddenly experienced difficulty in walking and was admitted to hospital for three weeks to undergo a number of tests. The doctors informed her parents of the diagnosis but nobody told Mary. The GP advised Mary's father not to tell her the full nature of the illness until a later stage. Mary was told by the doctors she had neuritis which was partly true.

As soon as others at church realised she was suffering, Mary was taken to all the local healing services. Everyone acted from good motives with Mary's best interests at heart and many people gave her a lot of their time. They accompanied her to every kind of meeting they could find and Mary was very pleased to go with them. There were all kinds of different styles from Methodist and URC to Anglican and Pentecostal. You name it, Mary did it.

As time went by everybody seemed to realise the true identity of Mary's illness except Mary. She met many others with the same symptoms as her, some suffering mildly and others in wheelchairs. The lady next door was one of those, but somehow the penny never dropped and nobody would say what they thought.

In her own quiet prayerful moments Mary was sure she heard God say he was going to heal her. During a personal quiet time she read, 'I am the Lord who heals you,' and it seemed to jump off the page. Despite this, about every six months a new attack would suddenly hit her. Her legs wouldn't work, she lacked co-ordination and her eyesight deteriorated. On one occasion she became blind in one eye for a while. Each time an attack came it was very distressing until it wore off a little later.

In between these bad moments there were many very good ones. Life was definitely not all bad news. Mary delighted in serving Jesus, worshipping him, going out with friends and helping people at work. Then, after seven years, the illness became worse and Mary was off work for three months. Eventually her mother told Mary the truth. 'You've got the same as Jacqueline next door,' she said.

Depression set in. Mary wanted to kill herself. Multiple Sclerosis seemed worse than death. She found it difficult to do simple things like picking up a knife and fork. She was frightened of being left alone, and kept thinking of all the possible ways of ending it all.

In a strange way, when Mary recovered from the initial shock, her relationship with God deepened and improved. As there was nothing any human could do to help she turned to God. 'There was nowhere else to go,' she said to me when recounting the story.

For a time the symptoms of the illness abated but then returned with a vengeance. After a session of prayer, people informed Mary that they thought her illness was a barometer for the state of their church. Mary felt quite chuffed. She was important and had a part to play in the spiritual life of the community. On other occasions things were said which at the time were encouraging. 'We need to stand against it,' Christian friends declared. 'Let's be positive.' Great power came upon her when two leaders laid hands on her head and she really believed healing was possible. One or two well-known Christian healing/evangelists had a go and afterwards Mary felt great for a short while. Prayer was usually appreciated and often helpful but improvement never became permanent.

As the years went by, Bible-reading continued to be a much-loved activity. When Mary was poorly again she remembered James chapter five and asked the deacons to pray for her. One of them asked, 'If Jesus was here and asked what you wanted, how would you reply?' When hands were laid upon her in Jesus' name, Mary saw a picture of herself completely healed and walking down the road. This gave her the answer for which she was looking. 'I'd like to walk down the road tomorrow,' Mary replied. After the prayer her disabilities once more abated and the next day she walked along the road on her own, albeit slowly.

Some time later a new pastor came to Mary's church who began to preach about healing. It was around this time that Mary started to struggle with the healing theme. Did she want to be completely healed or not? Eventually she asked the pastor for prayer and he laid hands on her during the morning service, commanding the MS to leave in Jesus' name. That afternoon Mary was able to stand up for forty-five minutes which until then had been quite impossible.

Mary was much better for a long time, but always felt she must push herself to do things, to prove that God was healing her. She took her orange disability badge off the car and sent her mobility allowance back to the social security. She took part in several 'Make Way' marches, feeling she should walk all the way. It seemed to be the time to exercise faith. There were no more major flare-ups for over five years and some people in the church spoke about Mary to others as the lady who had been healed of MS. But, as always, the symptoms returned.[1]

Eventually Mary came to our church and many of us prayed for and with her. On several occasions a number of demons appeared to manifest and be driven out in the name of Jesus. This gave us great hope.

Every time another big name came to Birmingham, Mary was encouraged to attend; every time we had a special healing service offering the anointing of oil or the laying-on of hands, Mary was helped to come forward; every time someone prophesied about great signs and wonders and healings which were coming our way, those sitting with Mary would nudge her and tell her to 'lift her faith'. Mary did her best.

On one occasion she thought the Lord was telling her to stand at the top of Burney Lane and run down the hill. We went with her. The spirit was very willing but the flesh was weak. We tried. We all tried. Mary tried hardest of all but to no avail, and we all went back in the vicarage for a cup of tea.

Mary continued to serve the Lord by teaching in the Sunday school and helping with some counselling. Following the visit of Billy Graham to our city she led some young people's nurture groups.

One day a visitor came to our church. He spoke about Isaiah chapter 53. Jesus bore our sicknesses on the cross, he said, and all we have to do is believe and receive our healing in faith and trust. This was too much for Mary. After nineteen years of promises, pain, pushing, prodding and prophecies she'd had enough. She hobbled out. Anger, resentment, hurt, rejection and most of all condemnation could be seen written across her face. I suddenly realised we had failed Mary very badly.

In our desire to see people healed so that we could tell their stories and encourage people to believe in Jesus, we had failed to show the compassion and mercy of Christ. I had never spoken about non-healing or how to survive as a sick Christian in a church with a healing ministry. I realised, almost too late, that many of our seriously ill church members who had been persuaded to attend big healing meetings in the city had been exposed to 'name it and claim it' theology. Now seemed to be the time to admit our blunders, redress the balance and address the problem.

Name it and claim it

Our visiting preacher put forward the popular view based on Isaiah 53:3–5 that Jesus bore our sicknesses in his body on the tree. 'All we need to do,' he said, 'is to believe and receive our healing. Jesus paid the price for all our illnesses at the Calvary Bank and we can draw on that investment with a cheque of faith. Just as Jesus died for all our sins on the cross so he also bore all our diseases. Name it and claim it in the name of Jesus and we will be healed.'[2]

This is a splendid doctrine for those who are well or who are totally healed as a result of responding in faith, and stay well for the rest of their lives. It must be said, however, that this is not normally a great percentage.

For those who are seriously ill and remain that way it is a doctrine of condemnation. When the beautiful passage about the suffering servant in Isaiah chapter 53 ought to be a solace and a help to those who suffer, it becomes instead a passage which accuses. If you are not healed it is your fault. Like Eliphaz, Bildad and Zophar, the accusers of Job, it meets the sick when they most need comfort with the brutal statement that they deserve their sickness.

It is a doctrine which can also lead to deceit and dishonesty. 'How are you today?' asks the pastor who believes any weakness or illness is the sign of a lack of faith. We quickly swallow the throat pastille, shove the handkerchief behind our backs, choke back the tears and with a smile from ear to ear reply, 'Fine, Pastor. Doing well,' and rush to the cloakroom to clear our throats before the service begins.

It must be very difficult being the pastor of such a church. If I catch a cold or need to wear spectacles I am seen to be failing. It must be almost impossible to attend such a church in a wheelchair. It is a doctrine which denies the need for any gifts of healing, 'words' from God or looking at the roots of a sickness with the intention of changing wrong beliefs or lifestyle. All we need is faith in what has already been done and we shall be well. There should, of course, be no use for the medical profession, either.

It is a doctrine which can lead me to doubt my own salvation. I am saved by believing in what Jesus did for me at the cross. If I am also healed by believing in what Jesus did for me at the cross, where does that leave my salvation if I am not healed? If I have not enough faith for healing what makes me think I have enough for salvation?

We need to ask if it is a doctrine which advances the kingdom of God. With those who are healed, most certainly. There is no sickness in heaven. With those who are not healed, it seems to be something other than the kingdom of God which is advanced. It can often afflict the afflicted, lead to deceit, encourage dependency on my faith rather than God's grace and thus cause me to doubt my assurance in God through Jesus. It would appear initially not to be a doctrine full of the compassion and mercy of God but of accusation, oppression and despair.

But is it true?

The New Testament

I have searched long and hard but as yet I cannot find any New Testament evidence to suggest we can be physically healed from all our diseases by having faith in Jesus' suffering—be it his stripes, his other wounds or his death. Healing in the New Testament appears to be seen differently from this.

Whenever Jesus received the authority of God the Father (Jn 5:19) and the power of the Holy Spirit (Lk 5:17) to heal the sick, people were healed. Sometimes they were all healed (Mt 12:15). Sometimes many were healed (Mk 1:34). In John chapter five many are sick but only one is healed. Sometimes no one was healed such as on Good Friday when three died. There is no evidence to suggest any were healed by Jesus before the Holy Spirit came upon him at his baptism. The people of Nazareth, including his own family (Mk 3:20–21), were surprised when he began his ministry (Lk 4:22–23). It seems likely Joseph had died by then (Jn 19:26–27).

When Jesus sent out the twelve to heal the sick he gave them power and authority (Lk 9:1–2), but he did not relate anyone's healing to his own suffering. After Pentecost, Peter, Philip and Paul were used by God to heal the sick but none of them did so by telling people to have faith in Jesus' stripes or cross in order to be healed. They healed people in the power of the Holy Spirit through the name of Jesus (Acts 3:1–10; 4:30; 5:12; 8:6–7; 9:17; 9:32–43; 13:18–19; 14:3; 28:8–9) and Paul went on to write about healing as a gift of the Holy Spirit (1 Cor 12:9).

The verses normally quoted to justify 'name it and claim it' theology are to be found in 1 Peter and Matthew chapter 8. 1 Peter 2:24 says, 'By whose stripes ye were healed' (AV) in the context of spiritual healing—the forgiveness of sins. There is no mention of physical healing in this passage. Matthew 8:17 says, 'He bore our infirmities and carried our diseases' in the context of Jesus' healing ministry. It is not in the context of the stripes, the cross or the atonement and no mention is made of suffering. I cannot find physical healing related to the atonement in the New Testament.

Isaiah 52:13—53:12

The Old Testament describes the punishment which will come to God's people if they sin—they will suffer. They will suffer disaster and sickness (Dt 28:58–59); they will suffer persecution (Lam 1:12,18); they will suffer death (Dt 30:17–18).

By the time Isaiah chapter 53 is written down all of these things have happened. But—following the extreme suffering of God's people in exile, 'double for all her sins' (Is 40:2)—a new message now appears. A suffering servant who is innocent (Is 53:9,11) bears these things for the others. He bears their sins (Is 53:11–12), their persecution (Is 53:5,7), their sicknesses (Is 53:4) and their death (Is 53:8,10). As a result they are healed (Is 53:5). This is a new idea and takes them by surprise (Is 53:4).

The language of this passage is entirely consistent with Old Testament atonement. The scapegoat or sacrificial lamb pays the penalty of sin so that the sinners may start again. More sacrifices are going to be needed again next year. Isaiah chapter 53 does not describe a change in the system, an alternative relationship with God or a new nature. It does not foresee the New Testament view of atonement which will end all sacrifices; it merely describes a different victim.

The clearest expression of this is found in Isaiah 53:10 where the death of the suffering servant is related to the guilt offering. 'The Lord makes his life a guilt offering' (Is 53:10).

John Goldingay commenting on this verse writes:

> The 'guilt-offering' or 'restitution-offering' was the means of getting right with Yahweh in such a situation of deliberate sin. The servant's life is offered on behalf of sinners in the way that an animal's life is offered according to the rite.[3]

The sickness and other forms of persecution which the servant suffered appear to be the punishment due to those who had gone astray (Is 53:6).

> Surely he took up our infirmities and carried our sorrows, yet we considered him stricken by God, smitten by him and afflicted. But he was pierced for our transgressions, he was crushed for our iniquities; the punishment that brought us peace was upon him, and by his wounds we are healed (Is 53:4–5).

The suffering servant seems to have been sick (Is 52:14, 53:2–4), persecuted (Is 53:5,7) and killed (Is 53:8–9) as a penalty for their sins. As a result they were healed. Thus the conclusion of the final two verses eleven and twelve, which says he bore their iniquities and their sins, appears to mean the innocent victim bore the penalty of their sins. This is in keeping with the Old Testament view of atonement. 'The punishment that brought us peace was upon him' (Is 53:5).[4]

Can we then see the fulfilment of this prophecy in Jesus? The New Testament suggests that we can. Matthew 8:17, Acts 8:28–35 and 1 Peter 2:24 all apply different phrases from Isaiah 53 to Jesus.

1 Peter 2:24 covers the bearing of sin and persecution: 'He himself bore our sins in his body on the tree, so that

we might die to sins and live for righteousness; by his wounds you have been healed.'

Matthew 8:17 mentions Jesus bearing our infirmities but not by being sick or suffering. The context is Jesus' healing ministry not the atonement. Does Jesus' death, then, have anything to say about physical healing? I believe two points are worth considering.

1) Jesus died for our sins, he payed the penalty of our sins that we might have eternal life (Rom 6:23). It seems right to suggest that if Jesus pays the penalty for all our sins, then whenever persecution or sickness are the penalty of sin, healing can be expected and claimed. Most Christians believe that Jesus paid the full penalty for sin not just part of it.

2) Jesus not only died for our sins, he also suffered for our sins. He was not just executed but he was also beaten, disfigured and marred beyond human likeness, pierced and crucified. He did not die quickly by bullet, noose or guillotine. He died because his body failed to heal itself over a period of several hours. On the cross he was not a well man.

Jesus suffered and died to pay the price for sin. As with the suffering servant of Isaiah chapter 53, it seems right to say that Jesus suffered persecution, lack of physical wholeness and death for our sins. I believe that whatever penalty sin carries, Jesus paid it for us. But we also need to note that according to the New Testament, Jesus did much more than bear the penalty of sin for us. He goes way beyond what people in the Old Testament had in mind. Paul writes: 'God made him who had no sin to be sin for us, so that in him we might become the righteousness of God' (2 Cor 5:21). Jesus becomes sin for us in order to deal with the whole root of sin. 'As in Adam all die, so in Christ will all be made alive' (1 Cor 15:22).

This is a new order, a new relationship; righteousness before God because of Jesus. There need not now be any more sacrifices. I have a new status. I am a new creation. I am an adopted son of God. All of these I receive by having faith in what Jesus has done for me on the cross.

The New Testament view of atonement is that Jesus became sin as well as bearing the penalty of sin. His once-for-all sacrifice atoned for all sin, past, present and future. He not only paid for sins already committed, he dealt with all sin so that all who believe might be saved.

'Name it and claim it' theologians argue that sickness is in the same category as sin. Just as Jesus dealt with all sin so he also dealt with all sickness. We need to ask if it is right to make this jump.

I have argued that in Isaiah chapter 53 the servant bore persecution as a penalty of sin and this is fulfilled in Jesus. But—Jesus says his disciples will still suffer persecution, because it is only the persecution due to sin that he bears. We cannot transfer what the New Testament says about sin to persecution. By what authority then can we transfer what the New Testament says about sin to sickness?

Bearing sickness in Isaiah chapter 53 is seen as paying the penalty of sin, suffering the punishment due to others. It seems right to suggest that Jesus did this. He paid the full penalty for all punishment which was due to us. But the New Testament does not develop the idea of bearing sickness as Paul and the writer to the Hebrews develop the idea of bearing sin. There is nothing in the New Testament to suggest that we can see atonement for sickness in the same way as we see atonement for sin. John Stott argues that the categories are completely different.

> Bearing the penalty of sin is readily intelligible, since sin's penalty is death and Christ dies our death in our place. But what is the penalty of sickness? It has none. Sickness may itself be a penalty for sin, but it is not itself a misdemeanor which attracts a penalty. So to speak of Christ 'atoning for' our sicknesses is to mix categories. It is not an intelligible notion.[5]

Jesus died for our sins, not our sicknesses. I believe sickness which is the penalty of sin can be healed through the atonement because at Calvary Jesus dealt with all sin, but I do not consider that we can claim healing for all states and conditions through the suffering and death of Christ. I can find nothing in Scripture to suggest that sickness unrelated to sin can be healed by faith in what Christ did at Calvary.

Those who believe and receive what Jesus has done for them can expect to receive the benefits of his passion. What then are those benefits? What healing is there in the atonement based on our understanding of Isaiah chapter 53?

I believe we can expect healing in three areas.

1) We can expect forgiveness of sins—acceptance by God—a restored relationship with God.

2) We can expect to be saved from the persecution and death which was due to us because of sin. We may suffer man's wrath; we may suffer Satan's wrath; but we need not suffer God's wrath.

3) We can expect healing from sicknesses which are due directly to sin.

None of these three healings are automatic. We are saved from sin and its penalties by believing in what Jesus has done, repenting of our sin, and receiving forgiveness and healing through faith in God.

The relationship between sin and sickness can be seen in Jesus' own ministry to the sick. Despite the example of Job, Jesus still saw some sickness as being connected to sin, while other sickness he sees as not due directly to sin.

When Jesus saw their faith, he said to the paralytic, 'Son your sins are forgiven' (Mk 2:5). To the man who was healed at the pool of Bethesda Jesus said, 'See, you are well again. Stop sinning or something worse may happen to you' (Jn 5:14).

Sometimes Jesus said sickness was connected with sin and experience bears this out. In my last book I wrote about a friend who, in middle-age, was suffering badly from arthritis. After she had accepted Jesus' death on the cross for herself and become a Christian, the Holy Spirit led Marie to forgive her mother. Once this was done there were no more signs or symptoms of arthritis. It would appear that the illness and the sin of unforgiveness were linked. The eventual 'shalom' which came to my friend through appropriating Christ's death on the cross included both spiritual and physical healing.[6]

James 5:16 also appears to link some sicknesses to sin. In the context of physical healing he writes, 'Therefore confess your sins to each other and pray for each other so that you may be healed.'

But—there were times when Jesus said that sin and healing were not directly connected. 'His disciples asked him, "Rabbi, who sinned, this man or his parents, that he was born blind?" "Neither this man nor his parents sinned," said Jesus' (Jn 9:2–3).

I am sure Jesus is not here attributing sinlessness to the man or his parents, but rather implying that the sickness was not due directly to their sin. Jesus then healed the man, a healing which was described by some of the Pharisees as a 'miraculous sign' (Jn 9:16). The healing of Vivian mentioned in chapter five probably comes into this category.

It would seem from Jesus' own ministry that sometimes there was a direct link between sin and sickness and sometimes there was not. This distinction gives us a way forward in seeking God's healing which is both sensible and biblical. We seek to apply the message of the cross to those whose sickness is due to sin. We pray for a miracle where it is not. I normally ask those who are ill and looking for ministry, one simple question: 'What was happening in your life when the symptoms first appeared?' Here are some of the answers which have proved to be helpful.

'I have had the pain in my right ear since we had drums

in church.' The young man who was suffering was the drummer. Church people had been critical. The ministry of forgiveness and affirmation led to healing.

'I have suffered pain through trapped sciatic nerves down the right-hand side of my body since my sister died.' As the lady began to release her sister, who was a Christian, into Jesus' hands, choosing life rather than death herself, the pain began to ease and eventually went altogether.

'I first noticed the cancer symptoms after I was promoted at work. I couldn't cope with all the strain and worry.' Her condition improved dramatically when the person gave the strain and worry to Jesus.

It needs to be said, however, that some sicknesses come to us as an indirect consequence of sin rather than because of sin itself. We need to be clear on the difference. A person may have lung cancer through smoking or develop Aids following an immoral relationship. Despite the way it seems, these illnesses are not directly due to sin. The lung cancer comes from smoke, not sin, and Aids is a virus. They are physical sicknesses due to physical means. It is the smoke and the virus which give the illnesses and not the sin. Innocent people who come into contact with cigarette smoke or the Aids virus may also become ill.

Jesus dealt with the penalty of sin at Calvary—he did not deal with the indirect consequences of sin. A murderer may find forgiveness of sins at the cross but it will not bring the victim back—that would need a miracle—the consequences of his sin remains. Similarly, we normally need a miracle to heal Aids or lung cancer.[7]

If sickness is not directly related to sin then I do not believe we can expect, as of right, to be healed because of what Jesus has done for us at Calvary. But it should be noted that healing in the atonement is not just limited to what Isaiah says about the suffering servant. Paul writes, 'And having disarmed the powers and authorities, he made a public spectacle of them, triumphing over them by the cross' (Col 2:15). Through Jesus' victory over Satan on the cross we now have the authority to cast out demons. As with Jesus' own ministry this can sometimes bring physical as well as spiritual healing. When I cast a demon out of a teenager in Malawi his sight was instantly restored.[8]

Paul also mentions the spiritual gifts of 'healing' and 'miraculous powers' (1 Cor 12:9–10). Because we are put right with God through Jesus' death on the cross we now have access to the same power of the Holy Spirit as Jesus received at his baptism and this power is sometimes present for us to heal the sick. When we prayed for Peter at Trelowarren, power came upon him and he was healed.

Jesus brought wholeness to people by casting out demons in the power of the Holy Spirit (Mt 12:28) and healing the sick whenever the power of God was present to do so (Lk 5:17). He received the authority of God the Father to heal the sick by doing what he saw the Father doing (Jn 5:19). Jesus also passed on to his disciples the same way of proceeding (Lk 9 and 10) and promised we could do the same (Jn 14:12). Physical healing connected to sin is limited to one or two verses in the Old Testament but the healing ministry of Jesus and his disciples, in the power of the Holy Spirit, is the oft-recurring theme of the New Testament. I consider that ministry in Jesus' name today should reflect this balance. But—we too can only do what the Father is doing. I believe sickness not related to sin can only be healed when God's authority and power is given for us to do so.

We live in an age when bodies still decay and die. There are signs of God's kingdom among us already, yet the best is still to be. Everyone who was present on the day of Pentecost in Jerusalem when the Christian church was born is now dead. Sometimes when the Holy Spirit comes he does a miracle and sometimes his grace is sufficient in our weakness.

I have met many Christians with a serious illness who

believe God is going to heal them. Some like Jennifer Rees Larcombe are wonderfully restored.[9] Others like Joni Eareckson are not.[10] Liberal theologians say they cannot believe in a God who heals some and not others so they don't believe God heals anybody. 'Name it and claim it' theologians say they cannot believe in a God who heals some and not others so they believe God heals everybody. If you are not healed it is your lack of faith. Reality is harder to accept but undoubtedly lies somewhere between the two. In Acts chapter twelve James is arrested and executed but Peter is set free by an angel. God can deliver us from all persecution just as he can heal us from all illness but he does not always choose to do so. He is God.

If a healing-evangelist preaches the cross and suffering of Jesus, some whose illnesses are directly related to sin may be healed. If demons are cast out in the power of the Holy Spirit at the meeting some more people may be healed. If the Holy Spirit is welcomed and God gives 'words', 'faith' to believe those 'words', gifts of healing and miracles then it is likely some more will be healed. And this is often what happens. At some such meetings some are healed. I have never experienced the signs following of everyone being healed nor do I believe it can be argued from Scripture. In John chapter five Jesus comes to a place where many were sick and he healed one man. Afterwards he said, 'I can only do what I see the Father doing' (Jn 5:19). This is the New Testament model for healing which I try to follow.

Conversations with many Bible-believing ministers leads me to believe that this uncertainty is one of the main reasons why they do not invite the Holy Spirit to move freely among their congregations. It is the insecurity of not knowing. If God heals nobody that is fine. We wait to be healed in heaven. If God heals everybody that is also fine. If I am not instantly made whole I know that a bit of work here, a shade more forgiveness there and I shall be healed like the rest. But sometimes 'yes' and sometimes 'no' means taking risks *every* time. It means I am not in control. It means I have to put a lot of time into listening to God and learning to trust him rather than myself.

This is a costly way forward. Compassion, love and mercy for those who are sick. Prayer but not promises. Ministry but not condemnation. I believe it is never wise to encourage people to have faith for a miracle unless we believe God is giving us a special 'word' to this effect. On the other hand, I consider it is always right to ask the Holy Spirit to come, to do whatever he wants to do, and to seek the wholeness, healing and spiritual oneness with God which is available through the blood of our Lord Jesus Christ. If Jesus is Lord then whatever he comes and does is fine.

So what of Mary?

Multiple Sclerosis is the deterioration of nerve ends. Physically speaking whatever has gone has gone, and what has been damaged remains damaged. The removal of several demons has not led to any major physical improvement.[8] If Mary is to be completely healed she needs a miracle. Having received ministry and counselling for nineteen years it now seems unlikely that Mary's sickness is due to sin. This means it is totally inappropriate to say to Mary have faith in what Jesus has done on the cross and you will be healed.

Mary is as aware as I am that sometimes God does do miracles, but life cannot be lived dependant upon that. When everything has been tried and prayed it is maybe time to accept life as it is, ask God for grace, come inside and close the door but leave a window open. We get on with life. But, if one day a breath of fresh air comes blowing in and Mary is healed, to God be all the glory.

The Holy Spirit brings in the kingdom of God which is a reign and not a realm. He helps us to know Jesus as Lord and to create a community where others may see him as Lord in us. For now this sometimes involves suffering. We can be free from the penalty of our own sin but not yet from the consequences of living in the world. It is important in learning to risk making mistakes for God that we learn to trust in Jesus as Lord and not in the circumstances of this life.

Endnotes

1. Christians from our area have, from time to time, taken to the streets marching for Jesus and singing the songs of Graham Kendrick's 'Make Way' marches. Graham Kendrick, *Make Way Music* (Kingsway Publications: Eastbourne, 1988).
2. I am aware that many so-called 'name it and claim it' preachers relate physical healing to the flogging Jesus received and not the cross. 'By his stripes we are healed' (1 Pet 2:24). This particular person spoke more of the healing we can claim because of God's covenant with his people sealed by the blood of Jesus. 'Healing', he said, 'is a covenant right.' I hope this section will be relevant to both claims.
3. John Goldingay, *God's Prophet, God's Servant* (Paternoster Press: Exeter, 1984), p 146.
4. All the commentators I have read agree that 'bearing sin' in Isaiah chapter 53 means bearing the penalty of sin. This is the natural Old Testament interpretation of such a phrase. A.M. Stibbs writes: 'To bear "sin" or "iniquity" means in the Old Testament to be answerable for it, and to endure its penalty, eg, to die (see Ex 28:43; Lev 24:15–16). This is the phraseology used in Is 53:12, "He bare the sin of many." '

   A.M. Stibbs, *1 Peter* (Tyndale Press: London, 1959), p 120.

   J.N.D. Kelly writes: 'In Is 53:12, "bearing sins" means taking the blame for sins, accepting the punishment due for them.... The implied teaching is that His sufferings and death were vicarious; as our representative He endured the penalties which our sins merited.'

   J.N.D. Kelly, *The Epistles of Peter and of Jude* (Adam and Charles Black: London, 1969), p 123.

   C.E.B. Cranfield writes: 'The bearing of our sins means suffering the punishment of them in our place' (cf. Num 14:33).

   C.E.B. Cranfield, *The First Epistle of Peter* (SCM Press: London, 1950), pp 67–68.
5. John Stott, *The Cross of Christ* (Inter-Varsity Press: Leicester, 1986), p 245.

6. The story of Marie is recorded in *Doing What Comes Supernaturally* (Kingsway Publications: Eastbourne, 1992), pp 207–208.
7. It may be more helpful to some if I illustrate this important point with a less emotive topic than cancer or Aids. If I am angry, bitter and unforgiving this sin may directly cause illness such as ulcers or heart trouble. My sickness is related to my sin. On the other hand if I trespass in my neighbour's garden to retrieve my football and in the process sting myself on a nettle, this sickness is not directly related to my sin. It is directly related to touching the nettle with an unprotected part of my body. If the owner of the house touches the same nettle while weeding the garden it is likely he too will be stung. Repentance, receiving God's forgiveness and forgiving others may help to heal the ulcers or heart trouble but the nettle sting is not directly related to my sin and therefore a dock-leaf rather than confession may bring more physical relief.
8. The story of Macdonald's healing is recorded in *The Hot Line* (Kingsway Publications: Eastbourne, 1990), p 255. We have found the presence of demons is sometimes directly related to illness. In this case the demon was probably sitting on the optic nerve or in some way limiting the young man's sight. Its removal brought instant healing. More frequently, however, demons assist in damaging the body like an intruder may damage a house. Remove the intruder and the damage remains. The body still needs to be healed. This seems to have been the case with Mary.
9. Jennifer Rees Larcombe records the remarkable story of her healing in the book *Unexpected Healing* (Hodder and Stoughton: London, 1991).
10. Joni Eareckson writes about her tragic accident and how God helped her to come to terms with it in her book *Joni* (Pickering and Inglis: Glasgow, 1976).

CHAPTER

9

Security, Identity and Worth in Jesus

If there is a more beautiful city in the world than Vancouver then I have yet to visit it. The 'playground of the Pacific' has a more temperate climate than most Canadian cities, allowing sailing craft of all kinds to use the extensive, ice-free, deep-water port all the year round. The marinas are as thickly forested with ships' masts as the surrounding countryside is populated with Duncan firs.

From any of its many beaches can be seen the dramatic high-rise skyline dwarfed by the Coast Mountains of British Colombia which end here on the North Shore. In places there are snow-covered peaks that rise to over 13,000 feet and are quite spectacular when viewed from the ocean. The cruise from Alaska to Vancouver is considered by many to be one of the most breathtaking in the world.

Orca whales play in the bay, spouting water at the ospreys that swoop low in search of salmon; bears and mountain lions come into the outskirts to investigate the garbage bins; chipmunks, squirrels of varying shades and a solitary skunk can be seen scampering about in the vastly wooded area of Stanley Park; and at dusk an occasional eagle soars high above the city, enjoying the thermal air-currents for one last time before diving down to shelter for the night.

In winter it is possible to catch the cable-car to the top of Grouse mountain or drive up to Cypress Provincial Park, spend the morning skiing and return to sea-level for a round of golf in the afternoon. Even in the height of a warm summer the snow-capped summit of the volcanic Mount Baker can be seen from various vantage points in Vancouver. Admittedly, the overhead cables are something of an eyesore, but the parts God has made are very special.

In the summer of 1992 I did an exchange with the Rector of Holy Trinity, Vancouver. On this occasion, unlike most of my other trips abroad, the family came with me. It was the first time in a jumbo jet for Amanda aged eleven; the first time flying over Greenland's icy mountains for Heather aged nine; the first time in America as we landed at Seattle for Hazel aged six; and the first time for Carol and me sleeping in a water-bed aged thirty-nine and a bit.

The circumstances of my life had never been better. I was thrilled to be taking my four most favourite ladies to swim in the Pacific Ocean and cycle by the water's edge around the harbour. I was looking forward to the arrangements which had been made for us to sail in the Georgia Strait and live in a luxury chalet among wild deer on the small island of Maine. I was excited at the prospect of driving the family on the road between the sea and the mountains, past the picturesque inlet of Howe Sound and the various cascading falls, on our way to the mountain resort of Whistler.

But so much more than this. I'd visited Vancouver before without the ladies and made many friends. I knew we would all enjoy the culture, the people, the church life and the checkout girls in the supermarkets who actually smile at customers.

I felt very secure about this visit. I was due to help with the services on six consecutive Sundays and old sermons would do. I am often very nervous about travelling distances and fulfilling speaking engagements because of the need to adapt to different cultures, but this time I'd already visited Vancouver and been put at ease by their warm reception. Americans often have to work very hard for a hearing in Vancouver but the English are made very welcome.

My writings had gone before me so on three Fridays and Saturdays I was booked to do day conferences. The fee people paid for coming on these would greatly help the air-fares. Again, the teaching material I'd already assembled for use on such days in England would do very well in Canada. People had been very accepting on my previous visit and I was led to believe the same would be true this time.

Who was I? I was to be the Rector of Holy Trinity, Vancouver for six weeks. Did I think I could do the job? I most certainly did. Would people thank me for what I had to offer? I was sure they would, even if only out of courtesy. My security was in the wonderful circumstances that now surrounded us. My identity was in the job I was to do. My worth was in the ability I had, the things I could do, and the expected praise of the affirming people for my efforts. The world seemed very good to me.

On the morning after we arrived none of us could sleep beyond five am. The eight-hour time difference gave us a head start over everyone else. Under a clear blue sky I drove the family through a deserted city to see Lions Gate Suspension Bridge stretched over the entrance to the harbour. The girls played in the sea and the large, free, open-air swimming pool nearby. 'Paradise regained' seemed to have come early.

The very next day I was not feeling quite so well. Jet-lag? Overdone it? Tickle in the throat—maybe a summer cold coming? By Saturday evening my head was full and my throat was sore; just what I needed for my first Sunday at Holy Trinity; great advertisement for the healing seminar I was doing five days later.

We prayed about it, came against it, exercised our faith and bought some decongestant tablets. As I waited upon God in preparation for the Sunday services I saw a picture in my mind of a cracked wedding ring and sensed it was a 'word' to be given out at the first service.

The following morning I was not feeling too good but I forced myself up, kept putting one foot in front of the other, prayed for help and took another tablet. I was due to speak at two morning services, and arrived for the first one just in time. I sat through the worship, sucked a throat sweet, coughed as quietly as I could and felt dreadful until I stood up to speak.

As I leant against the portable lectern an anointing from the Holy Spirit came upon me until I said my final word. There was no coughing, no need of the water and no throaty voice, but the moment I sat down I felt awful again.

Towards the end of the sermon I shared the picture I had received about the wedding ring. Afterwards several people came forward requesting prayer for marriage problems and I believe God came powerfully upon several of them, but I was looking for something else. On this occasion I was actually looking for a cracked wedding ring. I sensed earlier God had wanted me to give the 'word' ambiguously so that several people could be helped, but now I believed he wanted me to pray for the couple who had the cracked ring.

Between the services they came and saw me privately, showed me the ring, and I advised them to have it repaired. The couple were due to leave the church and take up a new appointment elsewhere having suffered from one or two difficult relationships. This was to be a sign of going in love with everything healed and God's blessing accompanying them. I prayed with them again on their last Sunday and asked God's blessing on their newly-mended ring.

The second service was like the first. I struggled until I preached and then everything was fine. As soon as the service was over I went home to bed. In the afternoon I endured a church barbecue kindly arranged to meet the Lawrences and then it was the water-bed for the rest of the week. It was important that I should be fit and healthy for my first healing seminar on the Friday night. I hoped nobody had noticed I was not too well.

The following few days were not unpleasant. I sloshed about on the bed, listened to Don Francisco on cassette, read a few Christian books and even contemplated writing one myself. 'Signs and Blunders' seemed a good title at the time. I prayed a lot—I always do when I need help.

By Thursday I was still unwell, not much worse, but definitely no better. We prayed all we could. Binding—cutting off—coming against—casting out—taking a stand—kneeling—sitting—standing—pleading—commanding—lying still and waiting. Nothing seemed to make any difference.

On Friday morning I was worse so I went to the doctor. I was given tablets for suspected flu. That must be it. The cold had been taken over by flu. Prayer, tablets, bit of faith should get me through. Maybe I'll feel better tomorrow.

Just after tea Carol went out with the children. It was the final session of the church's holiday club to which they had been going all week.

'I'll be OK,' I said. 'Just keep praying.'

But I wasn't OK. I seemed to be deteriorating by the minute. As I lay flat on my back the room began swirling round. I was dizzy and nauseous with a thumping headache. My brow was as wet as the inside of the bed. I felt very feverish.

Faith. Must try and exercise faith. God had brought me here to teach about healing. He didn't want me to fail or look foolish. I tried to stand but had to sit down immediately. I dressed as best as I could from a sitting position. I reminded myself of how God's anointing came upon me as I stood up to preach on the previous Sunday. Must get to the lectern. I forced myself up. Each step was more painful than the last. I gathered my things. The few yards to the car were like a marathon. Not much time to go but I opened the car and sat inside. No glasses. Everything seemed the wrong way round. Could I find the way? Traffic on the right-hand side. Would I still be alive when I arrived? Pain behind the eyes made concentration very difficult.

I don't know to this day how I made it nor how I smiled at the enthusiastic reception. 'Glad you've arrived. Worship's already started. You'll be on by eight.' I flopped in the chair. Where was the anointing? If only I can make it to the lectern. As people laid hands on me I became worse and worse. Nothing would keep still. The church was full. People had paid ten dollars to hear me speak and lead ministry sessions on healing.

The worship seemed to last for ever. The notices even longer. I staggered to my feet. Tottered to the lectern. Tried to speak but the anointing didn't come. I stumbled, knocked the water flying, began to fall and people caught me.

Doctors were there and helped me to the back. My friend Herbie had just been shopping and put a bag of frozen peas on my head. I thought this was it. The world was swirling round, coming and going, maybe ending. Some stayed to pray. Some were given their money back. We didn't sell many books that night. I was taken to hospital in an ambulance.

I lived in the belly of the whale for three nights and

three days. For three nights and three days I had no sleep. For three nights and three days my temperature remained at about 40°C, which I am reliably informed is several degrees too hot. For three nights and three days I was wired for drugs with great big bottles pumping stuff into my arm. After three nights and three days I'd had enough. I told a poor unsuspecting nurse what I thought about it all.

'I may not be a medic,' I began, 'but I do know these bottles are not doing me any good. If you gave me aspirin it would bring my temperature down, and if you gave me a sleeping tablet I'd get some rest.' At least that was the gist of what I said. I am very ashamed at how angry I was. We do not always know what is inside a cup until we bump into someone and it spills out. I was very upset afterwards thinking about what had spilled out of me.

The doctor came. He agreed. He disconnected me. 'We were worried you had something more serious,' he explained. 'We are sure now it is only Hepatitis 'A'.' I wondered why the mirror made me look yellow. Apparently it is often caught by eating contaminated food. As it takes three weeks for the symptoms to emerge I must have caught it in England. They gave me aspirin and my temperature came down. They gave me a sleeping tablet and I slept. I was back on the water-bed within another twenty-four hours.

For several weeks I was no longer the Rector of Holy Trinity. Others had to be brought in to take the services. For several weeks my circumstances were pretty awful. I did not really begin to feel strong again until the following Easter. For several weeks I gained no worth from what I could do or how well I could do it. I lay still and could do nothing. The security, identity and worth which I found in the world was suddenly taken from me.

Trusting in Jesus

Security

Paul says, 'I have learned to be content whatever the circumstances' (Phil 4:11)—and Paul found himself in some pretty grim circumstances. He was flogged, stoned, imprisoned, came close to execution more than once and yet his relationship with God through Jesus was never affected by what happened to him.

In Acts 15:39 Paul has a flaming row with Barnabas and they part company. Paul takes Silas with him instead. He tries to preach the word in Asia but is not allowed to do so. Instead he travels through Phrygia and Galatia from where he tries to enter Bithynia but meets rejection again. So he tries Troas, Samothrace, Neapolis and finally Philippi.

During this time Paul is on the road and the seas for days, weeks or maybe months without making any progress as a missionary. There was none of this one sermon and three thousand converted as Peter experienced first time out. There were no great crowds who were thrilled with the word and saw miraculous signs which Philip enjoyed in Samaria. After his bad row with Barnabas over John Mark, Paul meets failure after failure.

In Philippi there is, initially, a slight improvement. Paul stays a few days with a small group of women and one who already believes in God accepts what Paul says and is baptised. Unfortunately weeks of bad news have not sharpened Paul's discernment and he allows a fortune-teller to yell at him 'for many days' (Acts 16:18). Finally Paul twigs—and casts a demon out of her. Success at last! As a result of this they receive a severe flogging, are put in the innermost prison, chained painfully to the rat-infested floor and await possible execution in the morning. Who wants success?

It is now obvious what will be happening at midnight.

Paul is moaning, of course, about his circumstances. 'Lord, why have we been so despised and rejected? Is it punishment for losing my patience with Mark and my temper with Barnabas? Even so, Lord, months of fruitless toil, almost killed by the crowd, severely flogged, chained painfully to the floor, and now facing possible execution seems a little over the top for our misdemeanors. Why Lord? Why did the earlier disciples meet only success and we meet only failure?'

Actually the Bible records it rather differently. 'About midnight Paul and Silas were praying and singing hymns to God and the other prisoners were listening to them' (Acts 16:25). Paul's security was not in his circumstances. Paul's security was in Jesus.

Identity

Paul's identity was not found in his job, abilities or the role he played. Paul was a Pharisee—a Roman citizen—a tent-maker. He was a preacher and God did signs and wonders through him. He was an academic who could worship in Hebrew, chat to locals in Aramaic, write in Greek and preach to Caesar in Latin. But he never found his identity in these things. He used them from time to time—to be all things to all men that he might win some for Christ—but his identity was in Jesus. God had sent the Spirit of his Son into Paul's heart enabling him to cry, 'Abba, Father' (Gal 4:6). He was a son of the King.

Paul's identity was not in what he did but in who he was in Jesus.

Worth

Paul did not find his worth in what people said about him. He writes, 'When Peter came to Antioch, I opposed him to his face, because he was clearly in the wrong' (Gal 2:11). Paul was not a man-pleaser. He did not try to impress famous Apostles or leaders. He sought to obey God rather than men. He found his worth through Jesus who alone is worthy, not in the praise and affirmation of people.

Paul found his security, identity and worth in Jesus.

When I boarded the plane my *circumstances* felt as secure as ever. I came with my family to the 'second beautifullest city in the world' (according to Hazel who rates Birmingham as the tops)—fit, happy and full of eager anticipation because I knew the place to which I was coming.

My *identity* was clearly defined. I was to be the Rector of Holy Trinity. All I had to do was a couple of services on Sundays, two or three conferences, talk politely to one or two folks at a barbecue and I would be free to enjoy the sea, sun and mountains for the rest of the time.

Roger Jones, who has visited Vancouver several times, had assured me there would be plenty of nice people who would appreciate whatever I had to offer. I truly believed the people would endorse my *worth* as preacher, teacher and writer, even if they were only being kind.

My security, identity and worth seemed assured by my circumstances, my abilities and the acceptance of the community to which I was coming. But in a moment they were all wiped out. I felt like a clown, an idiot—useless and empty of self. This is the problem of finding security, identity and worth in the world and not in Jesus. The Lord is the same yesterday, today and for ever. The world often changes overnight. God is permanent. Circumstances, human abilities and opinions are transient.

Jesus warned his followers about this when he said, 'Do not rejoice that the spirits submit to you, but rejoice that your names are written in heaven' (Lk 10:20). In Luke chapter 9 the twelve had successfully cast demons out of some, but then failed totally with a young demonised boy. Our aim is not to trust in our ministry, nor in spiritual gifts, but in the one who gives them. Just as we are advised by Jesus to seek first the kingdom and not the signs, so we are warned about the dangers of finding security, identity and worth in those signs. Once more my own blunders brought me into a deeper relationship with God.

I prayed on the water-bed and God's power came upon me. He had not come when I cried out for healing, or for my circumstances to be restored, or to help me do what I thought I'd come to do. He did not help me to receive the praise I wanted from God's people, but he came instead as my Father.

I saw myself with Jesus, having the time of my life. We were hang-gliding, climbing, running, diving, swimming and riding on roller-coasters without any fear or dizziness. As I pictured Jesus in my mind I began to feel more secure in God and his plans for me. He told me I could choose virtually any fun activity and he would come with me. This was not quite the 'Jesus' I had always heard preached about from the pulpit, but the experience was so releasing. The Spirit of Jesus was reaffirming my identity as God's adopted Son. I started to receive worth through the Lamb of God who alone is worthy. I sensed great love, affirmation and healing from the encounter even long after the power and heat had faded away.

Today so many people seek comfort and security in circumstances: a louder stereo, a faster car, a bigger home. But there is no peace in the ever-receding horizon, even if we are successful. If I become bankrupt or unemployed then the roof falls in. So many find identity in what they can do, but if I find my identity as the best singer in the church choir, how do I cope if a better singer comes along and asks to join? So many look for worth in the eyes of the world or friends, but what happens if they love me enough to confront me with the truth, and where do I go when they let me down?

Security, identity and worth in Jesus is the only foundation which will survive the trials and tribulations of this world. It is my experience that when we find our security in circumstances, our identity in jobs and our worth in how well we do, then we are not very good candidates for a 'signs and blunders ministry'. Feeling safe in Jesus and knowing that our names are written in the book of life provides a much better launching-pad.

Recently I was booked to speak at a Saturday conference in Northampton. Two others from our church agreed to come with me even though it meant leaving at 7 am. I was also down to preach three times on the Sunday at home.

All three of our children were ill prior to the weekend and needed some time off school. On the Tuesday I was not very well; on the Wednesday I was proper poorly; on Thursday I was in bed. My feelings and actions became a total rerun of Vancouver.

We prayed all we could. Binding—cutting off—coming against—casting out—taking a stand—kneeling—sitting—standing—pleading—commanding—lying still and waiting. Nothing seemed to make any difference.

On Friday morning I was worse. Headache—full nose—sore throat—feeling dizzy and wobbly—just as before.

Earlier in the week I had read a book called *Only Love Can Make a Miracle* in which two of Mahesh Chavda's children had come within minutes of death through serious illness. Something he wrote kept coming back to me. 'God's ways are beyond our ability to comprehend. Don't become bitter. Trust the Lord, no matter how agonising the circumstances.'[1]

Mahesh and his wife, with tears in their eyes but no bitterness in their hearts, released both their children to God. At the very last moment both made sudden and complete recoveries. It spoke to me very deeply—not because both children were healed but because the parents could trust God whatever happened. I tried to release my own situation to God as well.

My symptoms did not improve at all, but God seemed to speak to me. 'There will be an elderly man present tomorrow morning with a sight problem in one eye,' I thought he said. 'Pray for him in front of the others.' My response was immediate: 'So I'll still be alive tomorrow?' I asked. 'You'll be fine,' God appeared to say.

I really didn't feel very well. It all appeared to me like a very hypothetical conversation. I did not think I would be in Northampton on Saturday or in our own church on Sunday. It seemed inevitable that more healing meetings would be cancelled due to the illness of the speaker. 'Trust me,' said God. 'How do I know it is you?' I asked. 'How do I know the "word" about the man at Northampton is right?'

'Simple,' replied God. 'If you're dead by tomorrow it is definitely wrong. If you are alive and coping, give it. Trust me.'

So I tried. The words of Mahesh continued to go round in my head. 'Trust the Lord no matter how agonising the circumstances.' I continued to feel ill but I didn't become angry or frustrated. In between dizzy spells I gathered notes together which would do for the next two days. I decided my security would be in God and not in the way I felt.

In the middle of the night I almost changed my mind. I couldn't sleep. I felt dreadful. I struggled to the bathroom and nearly collapsed. 'Trust me,' God seemed to say, 'It's going to be all right.'

Trust is not so difficult when asleep but I lay awake for hours. I had only just managed to doze off again when the alarm rang at 6.30 am. I arose, dressed, can't remember if I washed, shovelled in some cornflakes, had a hot lemon drink, grabbed my bag and made for the car. What a night! Strange though—I didn't feel quite so bad.

The sun shone. The morning was bright, fresh and frosty. There was hardly any traffic around and we arrived early. The chapel was very impressive. This is where Philip Doddridge was the minister from 1729 to 1751. This is where William Carey changed after being baptised in the local river. This is where I crept gingerly in, as I was now not feeling too well again. The worship leader invited us all to stand but I was unable to do so.

I flopped in the chair. Where was the anointing? Canadian thoughts reappeared. 'If only I can make it to the lectern.' The church was mostly empty. A few brave souls had paid to hear me speak and lead ministry sessions on healing. The worship seemed to last for ever. The notices even longer. I staggered to my feet, tottered to the lectern and tried to speak—and the anointing came. My head cleared, the dizziness went and my voice was strong.

After I had spoken I asked if there was an elderly man present with a problem in one eye. Out he came. Lovely person. All thirty who attended were delighted that God picked him out. We laid hands on his eye and power came on his hip. Funny. 'Why do you think that is?' I asked. 'Operation next week,' he said, 'Hip replacement.' Everyone was greatly encouraged by this to go on and receive for themselves. Many of those present were filled afresh quite noticeably by the Holy Spirit.

I continued to feel fine for the rest of the day. In the afternoon we retreated to a small room at the back and in a gathering of mainly elderly people I risked giving a 'word' for a lady with a gynaecological problem. I encouraged her not to see the monthly cycle as a curse and to thank God for being female. I received a detailed letter afterwards from a lady informing me how 'spot on' the word was for her. Her father had desperately wanted a son and she'd always tried to please him by being what he wanted, acting tough and playing with toy cars. She'd been seeing a specialist at the hospital for two years with serious women's problems. The 'word' itself was a great encouragement to her and confirmed the way prayer ministry had been going in recent weeks.

I slept better that night and was not too bad the following morning. All three services went well and the voice survived. I was tired on the Monday but very much at peace. The Lord had asked me to trust him and though I struggled at times he did not let me down. Sometimes when we trust in God we are healed, sometimes we are helped and sometimes he teaches us a new thing. When God comes he may change our circumstances or help us in them. Those who find their security, identity or worth in signs will often give up trying to minister in the power of the Holy Spirit when blunders come along. But those who trust in the Healer and not in the healing frequently receive more strength to continue in adversity. It seems good to me, if we are wanting to minister in the power of the Holy Spirit, to find our security, identity and worth in Jesus.

Endnotes

1. Mahesh Chavda with John Blattner, *Only Love Can Make a Miracle* (Kingsway Publications: Eastbourne, 1991).

CHAPTER

10

Blunders

We returned home from Vancouver via Los Angeles, Disney Land and Hollywood in the August of 1992. I was still very weak but managed to fulfil all my engagements by doing everything slowly. Whether it was due to living life at a gentler pace or not, God seemed to be very close to us.

In the October my wife Carol received a thought during her quite time. She sensed God was saying that 1993 would be the time to move. We had been at Christ Church, Burney Lane since 1979 so this was not totally unexpected. I asked God about it in my own prayer time.

'Yes,' he seemed to say, 'But you are not to look for a job, read the advertisements or begin applying for every vacancy you see. One will come to you by next Easter.'

Moving jobs, home and church is not a small matter. Many have been the thoughts in my head which I thought were from God that never came to pass. 'How will I know this is true?' I asked hesitantly.

'You will have a brand-new car by the end of the year,' God seemed to say, 'and when the job appears you will recognise it as right for you. It will meet all of your heart's desires.'

I shared this with Carol. We did not have much money in the bank and could certainly not buy a new car, however small. But believing it might be from God, Carol and I sat down together and agreed the specifications for our ideal job.

1) A place where the people would recognise God's call and anointing on my life. This is a difficult area. Many churches, when looking for a vicar, want someone to do what they want for themselves in a possessive kind of way. I desired somewhere that was willing to give me away to others; let me speak occasionally in other churches; even allow me to write books. I also wanted a group of people who would be prepared to let God have his church back and do whatever he wanted by his Spirit.

2) This meant I was not looking for a traditional second living: a) large desk buried beneath a mountain of paper; b) several curates to train; c) more than one PCC to run; d) church schools that needed the vicar to be a governor. Administration is not my gift.

3) But neither were we looking for an itinerant job. Our three girls aged twelve, ten and seven need a stable home for their teenage years with parents who are available to them. We wanted an area with suitable schools for the children and a church with lively youth work.

4) Living in a very pleasant four-bedroomed home where the girls each had their own room, we were looking for something similar.

I didn't dare mention such things as golf courses, cricket teams or the seaside; but Carol did say, 'Not London, please, Lord,' without telling me. We both agreed that no such job existed in the Church of England. Perhaps we had taken the phrase 'heart's desire' a little too seriously and selfishly.

My mother has lived in her house at Virginia Water since 1959. She never liked it—until Father died suddenly in 1977—then she said she would never leave it. Suddenly in the autumn of 1992, after God's revelation to us, we heard that Mum had seen a bungalow she liked and was thinking of moving. In the letter we received we were told the bungalow was £140,000 and her house would probably sell for £200,000. My mother wanted my sister and I to have the difference between us immediately. I wrote back thanking her for the generous offer and saying how much we needed a new car.

In the twinkling of an eye we moved from not being able to afford a Skoda to being in the market for a Mercedes—well, a small one. Unfortunately the estate agents valued mother's home at £150,000 so with commission, solicitor's fees and removal costs and dividing what was left with my sister, we were down to an old second-hand Skoda—which was not quite my heart's desire.

My mum wrote another letter to us mentioning that, despite the estate agent's valuation, she still wanted to help us buy a new car. We felt slightly embarrassed about this, but sufficiently encouraged to investigate the market. I went to the motor show in Birmingham. If mother was helping us to buy a car it seemed right to find one which had enough room for Carol and I, the three girls and Grandma (ill-health now prevented her from travelling anywhere unless taken).

Some cars in America have three seats in the front and three in the back but none in England do. It needed to be a seven-seater with three rows of seats. The cheapest I could find with forward-facing seats to avoid car-sickness was a Renault Savanna. A diesel model was available to help save on running costs and this would come to £10,500. We wrote to mother with these details but heard no more.

At the beginning of December I had a totally unexpected phone call from a solicitor. A church member who'd died earlier in the year had left us £9,900. To whom should he make the cheque payable?

I did a quick calculation. Six hundred pounds for our old car and we were there, almost to the nearest penny. I had been ordained over sixteen years and never received a phone call like this before: the exact amount—and such timing—I'd just be able to order it in time. It was the kind of story you always read about in other people's books. It sounded too good to be true. It was.

'Is the amount for me personally or the church?' I asked.

'Oh! For the church,' he clarified instantly. Of course. How presumptuous of me. It was just that having been to the garage the week before and....

The church needed it. It was a great blessing, which was very gratefully received.

We stayed with my mother after Christmas. She enquired how much we would need to help with a new car. Carol and I thought it through. Some money had recently arrived for book sales and speaking engagements. If we cleared everything we had out of all our savings accounts we could probably afford a new Renault Savanna diesel seven-seater, with a donation of £5,000. My mum is a very generous lady. We ordered our new car on 30 December and received it on 8 January. It goes beautifully and has already taken the six of us on holiday several times. As I write Mother's house is still not sold.

Was this the fulfilment of God's word to us? Some dear friends had been praying for us to receive a new car and they were overjoyed. We were not ungrateful. The impossible did seem to have happened but it felt a little 'man-managed'. We ordered it before the end of December but it only arrived eight days into the New Year.

Maybe it was some of God and some of us or a partial hearing, but we felt sufficiently encouraged to obey the rest of the prompting. I would not actively seek a job, or apply for one which had not first come to me, until after Easter.

We waited and waited during Lent for a job to arrive. My mother-in-law rang to say her vicar in Spain was leaving but I didn't recognise this non-cricket-playing, too-hot-to-move country as my special calling. A friend told me about a job in London and another one in Kent, but neither bishop saw me as the answer to their prayers when I wrote to enquire about them. And that was it. Easter came and went. Even after all the services were over on Easter Day, we leapt up when the phone rang with expectation in our hearts. The Outer Hebrides perhaps, or the Scilly Isles, or the beautiful island of Jersey? No, it was someone wanting to make arrangements for having her banns of marriage called.

We went to Spring Harvest with some members of our church and had a great time. There's nothing like close fellowship in a Butlin's chalet. We returned home determined to press on in the place where we were—there was in fact no other choice. A friend came to visit us. An Anglican clergyman whom God often uses powerfully, especially in evangelism. He'd applied for several jobs but not been offered any. 'There are not many jobs about,' he said. A friend of his had been for interview after interview—several times made the last two—never been given a job. Thus encouraged we plodded on.[1]

I was out when the phone call came; a gentleman married to one of the original Riding Lights. 'Must be getting on a bit now,' I thought to myself. Would we be interested in a job near Wimborne not far from Poole Harbour? I rang him back.[2]

'Why didn't you ring before Easter?' I asked abruptly.

'Pardon?' he said in a posh accent.

'God told us you'd ring before Easter,' I explained clearly to him.

'Oh, er...yes. Well, we hesitated a bit. Weren't absolutely sure,' he bumbled.

'I'd have said "yes" before Easter,' I continued.

Anyway, he came to see us to talk about it. New four-bedroomed house with two bathrooms, three showers, two garages, three loos and an attractive but small garden. The church gardener did the garden. Full-time administrator, two secretaries, four paid youth-workers, full-time lay pastor/evangelist. They wanted their vicar to be free from administrative worries so that he could have time to be what God wanted him to be.

Carry on, I thought to myself. This seemed to be moving in the right direction. Very good local schools including girls' grammar school where Amanda could transfer. A church that wanted to give away everything God had given them, and take teams to do weekends in other churches. And they wanted me. Someone to teach the 'how-to' when ministering in the power of the Holy Spirit. My name had come to several people when praying. One person had even received the name 'Peter' with an unusual middle name beginning with 'H'.[3]

It was a team vicar's job. No PCC to run. One in a team. The Team Rector was overall in charge but I would have a church called 'The Lantern' to look after.

The Team Rector invited us down. Carol had always wanted to live near the sea and loves sailing. The rectory and parish church are on the edge of the Canford School grounds beside the meandering River Stour and not far from the cricket pitch. The former home of Lady Wimborne looked majestic in its rural setting and I could belong to the golf club there for less than £50 a year. 'Yes, Lord,' I said, 'I think this is it.'

The Church Wardens wanted us, the outgoing Team Vicar thought it was right for us, the Team Rector wondered if we could start in September. We met some people from the Lantern Church and found them to be lovely Christians. We returned home on cloud nine.

On the Saturday my wife Carol went with our youngest daughter to visit her parents in Spain leaving me to look after Amanda and Heather for two weeks. On the Sunday night the Team Rector phoned me. Some members of The Lantern Church were not sure I was the right person for the job. Would I mind being included on a short list of four to be formally interviewed in a month's time?

I was devastated. I had never been interviewed for a job

in my life. I was used to speaking about Jesus not about myself. I thought of my friend and his friend and their frustration at being turned down at the final hurdle. I knew of a nearby church where eighty people had applied for the job of vicar and the one who was appointed presented a magnificent CV and interviewed splendidly. He had proved afterwards to be a disaster. The Team Rector who still supported me and tried to encourage me said I had undersold myself. I didn't think I was in the business of selling myself. For someone whose security, identity and worth should be in Jesus, I am disappointed at how rejected and upset I felt at the time.

Carol and I could not easily console one another on the phone. We suffered apart. Nobody would pick a football team based on interviews—you'd watch them play. Seventeen years of faithful ministry, in season and out, apparently counted for nothing. If I bodged a half-hour interview that was it. I wanted to say 'no' and crawl back to my little hole. I knew that my best chance had gone and I was hurting very badly.

The loophole in the guidance was the small errors. The car had not quite arrived by the end of the year even thought the eight days' delay made no practical difference to us. The job had not quite appeared by Easter although there had not been time to discuss and pray about what to do next before the phone call came. Everything else was perfect. The car was beautiful and economical with plenty of room for everyone. The people at The Lantern church were warm, affirming and had vision. The youth work was quite phenomenal and the en-suite bathroom in the modern vicarage was something else. There were just two small errors and my wounded pride in the way.

The next day I played cricket for the diocese and was out second ball for nought. This was bad news and good news. It meant a kind charismatic clergyman in our team counselled me all day in the pavilion. He knew the situation at The Lantern, he knew me and he knew the Lord.

His advice was very simple. 'This is a spiritual battle,' he said. 'Encourage as many people as possible to begin praying immediately.' He then listened to my moans and groans all day and still remained positive. His love and advice brought me back to a more even keel from where I could address the problem of the two errors. No matter how I felt, I needed to ask if it was God who was speaking and guiding or not.

Prophetic blunders in the Bible

The feeling of prophecy in the Old Testament is one of absolute certainty and accuracy. God said of Moses: 'With him I speak face to face, clearly and not in riddles' (Num 12:8); of Samuel it was said, 'All that he says comes true,' and virtually every Old Testament prophet felt confident in declaring, 'Thus says the Lord.'

Wayne Grudem has some interesting headings when writing about this subject:

> The prophets are messengers of God....
> The prophet's words are words of God....
> To disbelieve or disobey a prophet's words is to disbelieve or disobey God....
> The words of a true prophet are beyond challenge or question.

He entitles this particular chapter on the Old Testament 'Speaking God's Very Words'.[4]

Wayne Grudem argues each one well, supported by scriptural references. Perhaps the most telling is Deuteronomy 18:20—'A prophet who presumes to speak in my name anything I have not commanded him to say...must be put to death.' I wonder how many people who leap up to prophesy in our charismatic churches might be restrained a little if the same rules still applied today?

The Holy Spirit was not given to all believers under the Old Covenant, but when he anointed individuals with the gift of prophecy, they spoke with unquestioned authority and accuracy. There can be no doubt that measured against the Old Testament my two pieces of 'guidance' would be seen to be flawed. Although they were close, they did not come true. The car had not arrived by 31 December and the phone call had not come by Easter.

'If what a prophet proclaims in the name of the Lord does not take place or come true, that is a message the Lord has not spoken' (Deut 18:22).

When we turn to the New Testament, however, we find a different scenario. Wayne Grudem writes this: 'At first we might expect that New Testament prophets would be like the Old Testament prophets. But when we look through the New Testament itself this does not seem to be the case.'[5]

The beginning of the end or the end of the beginning appears to have happened in the life of John the Baptist. 'There is no one greater than John' (Lk 7:28) under the Old Covenant and he was 'filled with the Holy Spirit even from birth' (Lk 1:15). He delivers his prophecies and then when Jesus appears says, 'He must become greater; I must become less' (Jn 3:30). This appears to have happened. Not only is his ministry curtailed by being put in prison but his authority and accuracy also wane. Despite his earlier prophecies he now has doubts about Jesus. 'Are you the one who was to come,' he asks, 'or should we expect someone else?' (Lk 7:19).

John the Baptist is apparently the first signs and blunders prophet. Peter is very definitely the second. In Matthew 16:16 Simon Peter said to Jesus, 'You are the Christ, the Son of the living God.' Peter was right. Peter heard a message from God correctly. 'Jesus replied, "Blessed are you, Simon son of Jonah, for this was not revealed to you by man, but by my Father in heaven" ' (Mt 16:17).

Five verses later, 'Peter took him aside and began to rebuke him. "Never, Lord!" he said, "This shall never happen to you!" ' (Mt 16:22). This time Peter thought he was right, but was wrong. This thought did not come from God. 'Jesus turned and said to Peter, "Get behind me, Satan! You are a stumbling block to me; you do not have in mind the things of God, but the things of men!" ' (Mt 16:23).[6]

If ever there was a man who epitomises signs and blunders ministry it is Peter. Jesus gives him power and authority in Luke 9:1—an anointing from God—after which he declares God's truth and Satan's lies; walks on the water and sinks; draws his sword bravely and then denies his Lord. This is the leader of the New Testament Church.

In Acts chapter 11 Peter is asked to justify his action of taking the gospel to the Gentiles. In Acts chapter 15 Peter, Barnabas and Paul give further accounts at the council of Jerusalem on the same subject. The implication is that all are answerable to the church leaders and may at times be right or wrong. In Galatians 2:11 Paul writes, 'When Peter came to Antioch, I opposed him to his face, because he was clearly in the wrong.' These people were in at the beginning of the Christian church, filled with the Holy Spirit, healing the sick and raising the dead. Yet they knew in this present age they were not infallible.

In Acts 21:4 Luke writes: 'Through the Spirit they urged Paul not to go on to Jerusalem', but he went. Paul the Pharisee would never have disobeyed a 'word' which he considered to carry the absolute authority of God. This certainly seems to be something different from Old Testament prophecy.

A few verses later, 'a prophet named Agabus' gives another 'word' to Paul on the same subject. 'The Holy Spirit says, "In this way the Jews of Jerusalem will bind the owner of this belt and will hand him over to the Gentiles" ' (Acts 21:10–11). This time Paul not only fails to heed the warning but the prophecy can be seen to contain two small errors.

The fulfilment is recorded at the end of the same chapter. The Jews do not hand Paul over to the Romans but instead try to kill him, and it is the Romans, not the Jews, who bind him (Acts 21:30–36).

This is very encouraging. Someone else who made two small errors. Paul still ended up being bound and in prison as a result of going to Jerusalem but the inaccurate details would have caused Agabus to fail the Old Testament test. Here we have a third signs and blunders prophet.

Paul also found that the churches he planted very soon became signs and blunders churches. This is what he writes to them.

Paul says, 'Where there are prophecies, they will cease; where there are tongues, they will be stilled; where there is knowledge, it will pass away. For we know in part and we prophesy in part, but when perfection comes, the imperfect disappears' (1 Cor 13:8–10).

'Two or three prophets should speak, and the others should weigh carefully what is said' (1 Cor 14:29).

'Do not put out the Spirit's fire; do not treat prophecies with contempt. Test everything. Hold on to the good' (1 Thess 5:19–21).

The New Testament is not as full as the Old Testament with phrases like 'thus says the Lord'. The Holy Spirit has been poured out on all believers and the need to 'weigh', 'control' and 'test' messages from God has become very important.

It is strange in some ways to suggest that the coming of Jesus has made prophecy more inaccurate and yet the coming of Jesus to fulfil prophecy has definitely made it less important. Through the Old Testament prophets God revealed himself progressively to the Israelites. The prophetic task was to understand the nature and purposes of God not only so that his people would know his will for their lives but also that they might know him. Now God has revealed himself fully in Jesus, the prophetic task is much more one of guidance than of revelation. God affirms, assures and at times nudges us with bits of guidance and touches of power sufficient for the hour and the age; the age when faith not sight is still the doorway into God's kingdom. We see through a glass darkly rather than face to face, but we can now be assured of God's character because of his revelation to us in Jesus Christ as recorded in the New Testament.

It is sufficient for me to know that Agabus, approved as a prophet by the New Testament church full of apostles, could hear God, give God's helpful and preparatory 'word' to Paul and still make two small mistakes. I could not refuse to apply for the job at The Lantern on theological grounds. Signs and blunders are certainly biblical.

I took my cricketing colleague's advice. Friends in Cornwall and Southport began praying. A few dear saints at Christ Church also joined in the battle. They did not want me to leave and yet they prayed. I asked a senior clergyman in Birmingham to pray for me and he told me his son was on the short-list for the same job—but he also graciously prayed for me.

People at The Lantern and the other churches in the same team ministry prayed together and alone. One of the members of the leadership team, who was initially not sure I was the right person for the job, went down to the sea to be alone with God. The power of God came upon him and in a vision turned him right round. He knew immediately that I was the one who was to come.

But even if God speaks and people pray, the working out of God's purposes here on earth often involves our responsibility and hard work. I took to the golf course. My regular partner was a senior clergyman with vast experience at interviews. He told me all the questions they would ask me and how to go about answering them. Despite not being a card-carrying charismatic, his prophetic words came true. I was asked everything he said they would ask me, which was very helpful to a slow-thinking plodder like myself.

God went before me. I heard on the grape-vine about the other candidates who all seemed of a much higher calibre than me. Professional people from big churches; extensive CVs; sparkling interview techniques; Spirit-filled personalities with a gospel to proclaim. But the Lord cleared the path. Two of them accepted other jobs just before the interview date. The third candidate was a very gifted young clergyman but he hadn't been ordained nearly as long as me. I was eventually offered the post.

It is a lovely place and the people here are super. We believe God called us to be here. We believe God spoke to us about it and confirmed it with signs following. We believe God is with us, and loves us, and helps us to grow in grace even through pain. Carol now has her own boat and I belong to the golf club. Perhaps they are signs of God's kingdom too.[7]

On the third Sunday afternoon in my new parish, I sensed God's power come upon me and a challenge form in my mind. 'You keep telling them stories of what happened to other people in other places at other times. When are you going to do it here?' I knew exactly what he meant. Risk-taking is a good activity for 'yesterday' or 'tomorrow'. 'Today' is much more of a problem.

It is not easy to begin again in a new parish, especially when the predecessors have been gifted, successful, hard-working, well-loved and sadly missed. It is not a situation in which I wanted to make too many mistakes too soon and yet—when security, identity and worth are in Jesus—when we've met him at the cross....

'OK Lord,' I replied, after I had thought it through. Four 'words' appeared in my mind.

A woman with a thyroid problem.

A man suffering from muscle spasm.

A young person with a toe-nail problem.

A married couple with a hearing problem.

After I'd read them all out at the evening service a group of three people gathered at the front, one for each of the first three 'words'. Eventually Alan received prayer for the fourth one. He could not hear very well which meant his wife also had a hearing problem—ie, making him hear.

Alan and the lady with a thyroid problem both went over in the power of the Holy Spirit and afterwards Alan said he was hearing better. Mary was pleased to be picked out by God for prayer, being in the middle of a difficult financial situation, although the physical problem did not improve at the time. Ted had been suffering from tennis elbow for seven weeks and was greatly blessed by the ministry. We could see God's Spirit touching him. There was no immediate physical healing but all the symptoms went within a fortnight.

When I gave out the 'word' about the toe-nail problem a teenage girl with curled toes experienced great power coming on them. She did not come forward but as others laid hands on her afterwards she was partially healed. The young man with a toe-nail problem, who was pushed forward by his friends, made no improvement at the time.

These 'words' were not devastatingly accurate. Alan and his wife did not really fit 'a married couple with a hearing problem' though God's power certainly came on Alan. None of the other three were physically healed though various degrees of power and blessing were experienced by each one. Having somebody claim each of the 'words' ensured that I did not look a complete idiot, but neither did it make me look like Moses. But it was what happened afterwards which convinced me that God had taken the initiative.

People broke up into groups and we asked God for more 'words'. A young Christian who didn't expect to hear from God received impressions of a 'bandaged ankle' and a 'tooth problem causing headaches'. Both conditions were claimed in their small group to the amazement and encouragement of all present.

Close to me I spotted the church treasurer laying hands on an elderly Spanish man called Tony. As he went over in the Spirit the treasurer was heard to declare, 'It works! It works!' The man on the floor received a vision of Jesus who told him he'd been a 'naughty boy' but was now forgiven. This was a moving moment for him and brought tears to his eyes. As he was still lying on the floor with his eyes closed someone spoke from behind him. Normally Tony relies on lip-reading as he is very deaf but on this occasion he heard every word.

Dotted about the church were people resting in the Spirit—some moved to tears—one moved to laughter—and from another some demons moved out. The atmosphere was electric. God was among us. Ordinary people out there in the body of the church were having a go and God was blessing them. Sometimes when the guy at the front takes chances in God's goodness and grace, others are encouraged to do the same even if the leader does not get everything right.

Until Jesus returns 'we know in part and we prophesy in part'. One day, when perfection comes, the imperfect will pass away. Before it happens there will be times when God seems very close and his 'words' and power will bring extraordinary blessings to many people. On other occasions we will receive glimpses of God's glory in very earthen vessels when God's word the Bible and the body of Christ will be needed to sort out the wheat from the chaff. At different times from these God's grace alone will need to be sufficient for us in our weakness.

Some are healed and some are not. Sometimes we prophecy accurately, sometimes in part and sometimes in error. We 'who have the firstfruits of the Spirit, groan inwardly as we wait eagerly for our adoption as sons, the redemption of our bodies' (Rom 8:23). But we do not give up. Tasting the firstfruits encourages us to keep taking risks for God's sake and his kingdom. Believing who we are in Jesus gives us the security we need to take chances. Knowing that Jesus is in us gives us the power to enable others to taste the firstfruits for themselves. We may have the treasure in earthen vessels, but it is still a pearl of very great price and power.

Endnotes

1. Spring Harvest is a series of Christian meetings/holidays organised by the Evangelical Alliance and held at various Butlins' sites in the spring.
2. The Riding Lights are a Christian drama group who became well known when they accompanied David Watson on various missions.
3. The middle name of the Rev Peter Lawrence can be found in *Crockford's Clerical Directory, 1993/94* (Church House Publishing: London, 1993), p 408.
4. Wayne Grudem, *The Gift of Prophecy* (Kingsway Publications: Eastbourne, 1988), chapter one.
5. Wayne Grudem, *op cit*, p 25.
6. A shorter version of my thoughts on 'prophetic blunders' and the New Testament emphasis on testing 'words' from God first appeared in chapter four of my booklet *Explaining Hearing from God* (Sovereign World: Tonbridge, 1992).
7. In 1994 I was appointed Team Rector of the parish, but allowed to remain attached to the Lantern Church.

CHAPTER

11

Walking Dynamite

Dorset is the land of thatched cottages, steeply-inclined cobbled roadways, quaint villages, limestone cliffs and chalk downs. Nature's sculptors have carved deep chines down to sandy shores where some of the rocks which rise from the sea bed have been carved into abstract shapes and forms far superior to anything found in the Tate Gallery. It is a place where it is only too easy to get away from it all; far from the madding crowd.

Here, beside the whitewashed dwellings of the little port, Jane Austen's Louisa Musgrave fell from the breakwater; here Thomas Hardy's *Casterbridge*, *Budmouth* and *Sherton Abbas* can be found if one only knows their true identity; here T.E. Lawrence lived in a cottage known as 'Clouds Hill' at the end of his life.[1]

This is also the area where rural poverty is rife, many young unemployed people are addicted to drugs and the farmers suffer from a high rate of depression and suicide. We were called here in 1993. Johnny came three years earlier.

At the age of twenty-two he was appointed as Youth Worker to our group of churches, inheriting a small group of teenagers. Trained by YWAM, Johnny decided to shut down the existing structures and take time to assess the situation. A Sunday night social group was formed instead in order to maintain links with the young people.

Johnny removed the doors which divided the lounge from the dining room in the house provided by the church, visited the local tip and filled the place with old dilapidated furniture. The youngsters seemed to feel comfortable in such a setting.

Some of the former leaders were still keen to be involved so God was invited to sift them. Johnny talked to the volunteers about the cost of commitment and started a fasting and prayer rota. He spent all his time doing an audit of the area. He visited the pubs, walked the estate and studied the local history at the library. Our estate has about six thousand people living on it and most of the houses are privately owned. It was built on an old aerodrome beside the village of Canford Magna in the late sixties/early seventies to provide housing for the employees of expanding businesses in Poole. Apathetic materialism seemed to be one of the major strongholds to come against.

Alun and Debbie were the two leaders whom Johnny chose to act as his right-hand people. They were invited for breakfast at 6 am to discuss what God had been saying during the time of fasting and prayer. What emerged from the discussions was a unanimous joint desire to hold meetings for the unchurched.

The small village of Canford Magna consists mainly of Victorian red-brick cottages where tall chimneys are the order of the day. A number of the dwellings belong to the Canford public school including one with a newly-replaced thatched roof. Situated at the end of this row of old English dwellings stands a village hall belonging to the Diocesan Education Board. Johnny went to the PCC and asked for five hundred pounds with which to do it up and permission to hold meetings in it. There were long and hard discussions. The problem was not with the Diocese or in finding the money, the problem was whether to fire Johnny or not!

The new youth leader had been there three months and all he'd done was close down the existing structures. There was much to discuss. If we were paying someone to change the world in three years would we think we were receiving value for money if he spent the first forty days praying and fasting in a desert? It was a close decision. Johnny stayed and was given the £500.

By now the social Sunday night group had grown from eight to forty. Evenings were spent relaxing around outdoor log fires, leaping about at discos, or mooching about in The Lantern. The leaders tried to take them to the liveliest Christian celebrations they could find, but like my similar attempts with the Birmingham youth, these had not been a success.

Secular activities worked better. The 'raves' provided one access point which attracted scores of young people. Whole evenings were given over to a certain style of music. The first of these was planned with tickets, posters, and word-of-mouth advertising which initially took the organisers way out of their depth. Weirdos turned up from everywhere, on bikes and in camper-vans. Two hundred came bringing drugs, alcohol and weapons of various descriptions. Johnny and co. summed up their naivety with an apt phrase: 'We learnt by being burnt'.

Before the next event took place, a team was trained in security ready to search everyone when they arrived, and the leaders attended a lecture on the drug scene. Rules were made and displayed. 'No snogging and groping. No drugs and alcohol. No weapons'. Everyone was shown the rules when they arrived, which declared their right to refuse admission and to search everyone before being allowed in. The early disaster was turned into a success. They became instantly known, the rules were soon accepted, and the show was up and running once a week.

The refurbished village hall was called the 'Night Bin'.

They spiced it up to look youth friendly and the social group agreed to move from Johnny's 'tip' to the 'bin'. They hung up some strange pictures, dimmed the lights and dotted a few pool tables here and there in the alcoves. A programme was produced. A gifted artist was found and a very impressive glossy brochure emerged from his efforts. Every four weeks there were to be two talks on young people's issues from a Christian perspective, one evening of testimonies and one evangelistic session. These took place on a Wednesday night with the 'raves' on a Friday. The Sunday evenings became a follow-up to the Wednesdays while continuing to act as a social pick-up point.

It must be said that the glossy brochure did not communicate the Christian programme in an obvious way. Film titles were used to describe the talks on young people's issues such as: 'Fatal attraction', 'When Harry met Sally' and 'Sex, lies and video tape'. As a result the meetings were well attended but no one complained.

The happenings brought Johnny and his leaders into contact with the local young people in a non-threatening, youth-friendly atmosphere which now included some Christian content. But I doubt whether this contact on its own would have led to much fruit were it not also for the coming of the Holy Spirit. The whole work was soaked in prayer by those immediately involved and supported by members from the local group of churches. The structures were in place, the meetings going ahead, but it was the power encounters which made the spiritual difference. I am convinced God brought these about in response to prayer, fasting and spiritual warfare. The first one came about by discerning God's activity in the middle of difficult circumstances and taking the opportunity.

As Johnny became accredited in the eyes of the local youth, they began dropping into his 'tip'. Anybody and everybody was welcome at all hours. On one occasion three lads who were into hard-core music dropped in and drank coffee in the kitchen. Welcoming them was one thing, but getting rid of them proved to be quite another. It was only long after the youths had outstayed their welcome that an idea came to the legal tenant.

'You'll have to go now,' said Johnny, 'I'm about to have my quiet time.'

'What's that?' enquired the three musketeers.

'It's when I speak to God and he speaks to me,' replied our youth leader. The enquirers tried to control themselves but failed. At first they fell about laughing and then one of them cursed quite badly. Johnny felt deflated.

'God's here right now,' he said. There was a moment's pause. There was more laughter. 'Will you say one for me?' the visitors asked in turn. They sounded lighthearted and cynical. Johnny's answer was serious.

'Yes,' he said, 'on one condition. I'll say one for each of you providing you are prepared for God to speak back to you.' They agreed and left. Johnny was pleased to see them go having been made something of a laughing stock not knowing that his three friends had concealed what was really taking place.

As they left the 'tip' one of them said to the others. 'Did you feel that? When he said God's here right now? Something nearly pushed me over. I had to hang on to the kitchen unit to stop myself falling on to the floor.'

All three had felt the power of God but refused to let Johnny see what was happening. In the quiet time which followed Johnny said one for each of them.

'Lord,' he prayed, 'what would you like to say to Lee?' God told him. Impressions in the mind. Johnny wrote it all down. He did the same for Matt and Jo.

After the next meeting Johnny gave the three of them a lift home in his van. As they stopped at Lee's place Johnny handed him an envelope. 'This is for you, Lee,' he said, 'from the Lord.' As he handed it to him power came upon the two sitting in the back and this time they began to shake.

Lee took the envelope, began walking away and then came back. He knocked at the window. 'What happens if he talks to me?' he asked with some trepidation. This was a bigger force than he'd met before. Johnny reassured him, giving advice about the God of love who could be invited to come into his life through Jesus, or be kept out by saying 'no'.

At home he opened the envelope and read the words. How did he know? he kept asking himself. How did he know what my life is like, what I'm thinking, what I'm feeling? He went to speak to his parents who themselves were in the process of becoming Jehovah's Witnesses. Lee asked them if they minded him becoming a Christian. They gave permission and Lee asked the Lord Jesus Christ to come into his life and save him. Peace and power entered his life.

Meanwhile the other two were still shaking in the back of the van. 'Got one for me?' they both asked in a wobbly kind of way. Incredible power kept going through them both until four in the morning. The only way they could describe it was like being high on speed without any after-effects.

The words on both pieces of paper were as accurate as the ones Lee received and spoke right into the heart of their differing situations. Matt couldn't cope. He ripped up the paper and flushed it away, went home but failed to get much sleep. He moved from being agnostic to believing in God but he did not, at the time, make a commitment to Jesus Christ.

Jo, on the other hand, started coming to The Lantern Church, had regular chats with Johnny and others and eventually went forward to ask for prayer. This began a real move of God's Holy Spirit among the young people.

One of them, hearing the word preached and the testimonies, said to God, 'Whenever you wanna say "Hi" that's all right by me.' He lived in a caravan. At four in the morning he was woken up suddenly feeling as if the whole place was on fire. Once he'd adjusted to the brightness and the awesome feeling of power and love all he could say was, 'He's come.'

Joss spoke to Johnny in his van. He was having bad nightmares and wanted help. Johnny knew he was into occult practices. 'You are being tormented by an evil spirit,' he said calmly. This was appropriate and acceptable language to Joss. 'What shall I do then?' he asked.

Johnny advised him to give up all his occult practices and then offered to pray for him. 'But,' he warned, 'it may happen again unless you can get yourself into a safe place.' Joss wanted to be free and in a safe place so Johnny explained to him how he needed to be hidden in Jesus. Joss listened and then said, 'Yes.' He wanted to be safe. He invited the Lord Jesus into his life. Johnny gave him illustrated versions of the Bible and the story of Nicky Cruz. Joss suffered no more nightmares.

In one of their meetings Rob was suffering badly from a migraine. As the leaders laid on hands in the name of Jesus the migraine went completely and everyone witnessed the difference. Des was booked into hospital for an operation on his gammy knee. Hands were laid on him and he too was healed in front of the others. The operation was never needed.

Steve started coming as a result of attending several 'raves'. After one meeting he came forward to have a word with Johnny. 'I am psychic,' he said, 'I often receive accurate information about future events.' Steve was from gypsy origins. On one occasion he predicted with great accuracy a car accident which happened to his grandfather. He named the person, the place and the time with precision.[2]

When Johnny asked him how he did it Steve told him about a spirit that often led him and gave him predictions. God seemed to give wisdom to our youth leader.

'Have you heard of the Holy Spirit?' asked Johnny.

'No,' replied Steve immediately.

'He is the most powerful Spirit,' continued Johnny, 'and the most loving. He saves, heals and always does good. He is the Spirit who belongs to Jesus.'

'It's funny,' said Steve, 'but I don't really know my spirit. He's not with me all the time.'

'The Holy Spirit,' explained Johnny, 'has a personal relationship with me. He's with me all the time. Your spirit wants to control and possess. The Holy Spirit only wants to love and care.'

'That's what I want,' responded Steve, 'How do I get him?'

Johnny thought for a moment. At this point it was feeling very much like Simon the sorcerer in Acts chapter eight. If he offered the Holy Spirit for a fiver Steve would take up the offer.

'There's one condition,' proceeded Johnny cautiously. 'The Holy Spirit and the other spirits don't get on too well. It's one or the other. When we confess Jesus as Lord, and no one else, then the Holy Spirit will come in. He brings good and not bad. We have to choose good or bad. He sometimes gives premonitions too, but only for good. You will have to choose.'

Steve did not even have to think. Sometimes when people have experienced the reality of the kingdom of darkness they understand the choice better than anyone else. 'I want Jesus,' he said in a definite manner. 'How do I get him?'

'Ask him in,' said Johnny simply. 'Say "no" to the family spirit and "yes" to Jesus.'

This was the crunch and for the first time Steve was hesitant. 'How do I know the Holy Spirit is the most powerful?' he enquired. 'Ask him to show you,' said Johnny, 'and make up your mind after that.' Often when we try to share the gospel we trust in our words rather than in God. Sometimes to challenge people to ask God, if they really mean business, to come to them in ways they can understand is the more helpful approach. Steve said, 'Yes.'

Johnny invited the Holy Spirit, the Spirit of Jesus, to come on Steve. He came almost immediately. Steve experienced great surges of God's power and stayed there for some time. When he eventually cooled down he was sparkling. His eyes were clear and bright. 'Wow!' he said, 'Is that the Holy Spirit?'

'That's just him on the outside,' explained Johnny.

'Yeah?' he asked, 'I need Jesus then. I want him on the inside.'

'Then you'll need to let go of the family spirit,' challenged Johnny.

Steve renounced his former ways and the family spirit and asked Jesus to come into his life, by his Holy Spirit. He came and he's still with him.

On the same night a girl called Michelle came to the meeting. She had also been reached through the 'raves'. While others made commitments to Jesus, she held out. Michelle was a 'tough cookie'. Very street-wise; always scowling; mouth edges permanently turned down; forever ready to bite someone's head off given half a chance.

Following a challenge from the speaker, Michelle asked Jesus into her life in a quiet corner. Johnny didn't know it had happened but bumped into her later. She looked like an angel. There was a smile on her face and her eyes had come alive.

'Hey,' said Johnny. 'Something's happened to you. Have you become a Christian?'

'Yeah,' said Michelle with enthusiasm, 'Tonight.'

As with the Birmingham four and the Ireland eleven, the youth leaders in Canford have witnessed God's response to much prayer and careful planning. As I write there are one hundred and eighty young people in cell house groups training to be disciples of Jesus Christ. To God be all the glory.

When we read about unbelievers shaking under the

power of the Holy Spirit or accurate 'words' from God speaking right into a non-Christian's situation, we are often amazed, sometimes thrilled, but nearly always surprised. We do not expect it. It is not normal. And yet the New Testament seems to suggest it ought to be more normal than we think.

The Holy Spirit lives inside every born-again believer. This is the same Holy Spirit who moved on the face of the deep in creation. He is the one who gave wisdom to Solomon, strength to Samson and enabled David to kill Goliath. He it was who came on Jesus at his baptism before he did any signs and wonders, helping him to defeat Satan and all his works.

This is the same Holy Spirit who enabled the early disciples to carry on doing the works of Jesus and speaking his words. This is the Holy Spirit who gives all Christians access to the mind of Christ, the power which raised Jesus from the dead, convicts the world of sin and judgement and helps us to cry, 'Abba—Father.'

I don't think many of us in Britain have begun to grasp the significance of who is inside us or to tap his resources. We are walking dynamite. Despite what I have just said—all of which those of us who are Christians probably know already—most of us choose most of the time to do things our own way. And look at us. Our lives. Our church. Our nation.

Leanne Payne speaks of 'practising the presence of Jesus'. But despite the obvious common sense in this I spend much of my time practising the presence of Peter. Most of my life people have not been slow to criticise me—to moan about the pain my presence causes them—and they only have to put up with me for a few minutes a week. I have had to live with me all my life. How do they think I feel? It makes sense to practise the presence of Jesus rather than the presence of Peter. Those are the two very real choices I have at any moment of any day, in any circumstances.[3]

Why is it that I am sometimes down, occasionally depressed and from time to time think that life is not all that great? Because I am concentrating on me. I think of the things I've bodged. The people I've upset. The tasks I've failed to accomplish. The dream I had when I was young that disappeared under the thick catalogue of disasters which filled the subsequent years. It is hardly surprising I am depressed if I think of me.

But if I think of the Jesus who is in me I enter a whole new world. The walk to the letter-box can turn into a great adventure. I might come across a thirsty woman at a filling station and tell her all kinds of things about herself. I could meet a man with no guile, or see a little rich guy in a tree, or heal a person with a bad leg standing at the bus-stop. I may even find someone in the back of a chariot reading John 3:16 while waiting at the traffic lights. Maybe he would ask me what it means and I would....

With God all things are possible. Practising the presence of Jesus rather than self gives us all the opportunity of leading people out there in the world to salvation in Christ, but it frequently involves having to risk mistakes.

One day I caught the train from Eastbourne to London on my way to Birmingham. My eldest daughter Amanda was with me. I enjoy taking one of my daughters with me on ministry trips whenever I can and the time together in the train, playing Ludo and other games, was very special. Then it happened.

'Peter, I want you to minister to that lady sitting over there.' It was an unwelcome and intrusive thought. I couldn't see how it was possible. Excuse me, madam, but I think the Lord is saying...! Others might be able to manage such intrusions into people's privacy on trains but I certainly could not. Even so, I kept my eye on her during the rest of the journey.

Seated alone on the other side of the aisle, this rather overweight, middle-aged lady smoked continually and did seem to be registering some sort of distress on her face. Half way to London she fell asleep. While she was in this position a man boarded the train and took his seat opposite her. As he did so she opened her eyes with a jump and looked 'daggers-drawn' at him for a moment. After she closed her eyes again, I smiled at the man and we both shrugged our shoulders in recognition of one another's puzzlement at the incident.

If a 'word' comes to me in a meeting and it seems appropriate I give it on the spot. Always introducing it with phrases such as, 'forgive me if I'm wrong but...' or 'as we were worshipping I wondered if the Lord might be saying....' It is then normally claimed or not and the whole incident has come and gone in five minutes. A possible 'word' on a train is a different matter. As the wheels rattled over the lines and time passed by, the journey became more and more uncomfortable.

'Daddy, it's your turn again—you're not concentrating...don't you want to play Ludo with me?' demanded a frustrated young lady.

'Oh...er...yes...of course dear. I still need a six don't I?'

How could I minister to her? Forgive my intrusion, Madam, but would you mind standing up while I just lay my hands on you?

Amanda's counters all arrived safely home while most of mine were still at base camp. We paused for a breather. We'd be there soon.

'Lord, just supposing this thought was from you,' I prayed, 'what should I do? It just doesn't seem possible.'

'Trust me,' he said, and that was all.

Now if he'd given me a message to pass on or even a conversation-starter, I could maybe have a go. I saw you under the fig tree...or...the man you're living with is not your husband—or been up any good trees lately? But I couldn't seem to find out anything more from God whatsoever even though he didn't seem to be sharing my anxiety.

As we approached Victoria Station I instructed Amanda as clearly as possible about the tube to Euston, just in case we were accidentally parted. We had plenty of time.

The train came to a halt and I found myself standing next to the lady as we both sought to retrieve our baggage from the rack. 'Are you all right?' I asked nonchalantly and the lady obviously felt the need to explain the incident with the other passenger. She was suffering badly from a trapped nerve in her back and the man had apparently just caught her foot while sitting down. Being at full stretch, she was then woken suddenly as excruciating pain shot up the right-hand side of her body.

I commiserated, helped her off with her bags, and then turned my attention to Amanda and our suitcases. As we alighted from the train the lady was struggling some distance ahead, obviously in pain. Needless to say there were no porters or trolleys to be seen.

Thoughts raced quickly through my mind. A man cannot easily approach a woman he has never met before, on Victoria Station, offering to pray for her. No, of course not. Especially as I was not wearing my clerical collar. And yet there were extenuating circumstances. We had been in a train compartment together for over an hour. We had spoken. The platform was a public place and I did have my daughter with me. This seemed to make a difference. She had seen me relating to my daughter for much of the journey and I instinctively felt in this situation it would be possible. Somehow having Amanda with me made the whole idea of ministering much more within the bounds of social acceptability.

I asked the Lord what he thought. He had not changed his mind. I thought it might be appropriate, having now already spoken to her, to say, 'I'm a vicar, as you're in pain would you like me to pray with you?' I could then hold my hand a few inches from the affected area and pray. There was still plenty of time before our train departed from Euston.

More thoughts jostled each other for prominence in my head as I suddenly realised I was well prepared for this moment. I am not often used for healing the sick but I had previously prayed with three people in church with exactly the same condition as this lady. Two had been instantly healed and one had received much relief. The Lord did appear to have the right man on the spot! It didn't really matter if she was completely healed there and then as long as power came on her and she received some relief or positive experience in the name of Jesus. There were follow-up possibilities as well.

It so happened I had a few covers of one of my books in my briefcase. If I gave her one this would tell her who I was, encourage her maybe to buy and read the Christian book, or perhaps write to me as my name and church were on the cover. I would then tell her all about Jesus and even suggest a nearby church. It was a situation with great potential. It is quite amazing how God can set up a divine appointment like this out of nothing.

We so often doubt God. We say, of course, it is not God we are doubting but our own ability to receive or hear correctly. Nudges, thoughts, premonitions come and go because we are not quite sure. We don't want to get it wrong. We don't want to let God down. But what an amazing sequence of events I was now witnessing. A lady in the same compartment—a thought—a man who catches her foot—an explanation—a condition I have prayed for on three other occasions all with some degree of success—time at our disposal—a chaperon with me—and someone clearly in distress who would value any kind of help at all. This had to be God. The living God who lives inside us. The God who speaks. The God who also comes to act upon what he has said. I had done virtually nothing at all and God had set up the appointment. I could hardly fail.

About twenty yards in front of me she stopped, put her bags down and held her painful back. I approached her gently, now knowing full well what God wanted me to do.

'Still having trouble?' I asked.

'Yes, I'm in agony,' she said. 'I don't know how I'm going to cope. I've still got to catch another train.'

'Oh dear,' I said. 'I am sorry. Hope you manage,' and went by on the other side.

'Thanks,' she said.

Amanda and I walked on and left the lady behind with her bags and her pain. At least she didn't know I was supposed to be a Christian.

It was now the middle of the rush hour. Amanda and I had only a couple of square inches to share between us on the underground platform as the sardine tin thundered to a halt in front of us. 'This is ours,' I said triumphantly without anticipating the problem. Before I could stop her Amanda had darted in and out of the legs, through the open doors of the tube train, and buried herself among a mass of human bodies none of whom seemed to be alighting at Victoria. It was simply not possible for the people on the platform to fit into the already overcrowded carriages. The London Underground official realised this and pushed the button to close the doors.

Somewhere in the middle of this train was my daughter while I was still squashed in a scrum six feet from the train, unable to move. I panicked. I never played rugby at school but I had been quite good at British Bulldog in the Boy Scouts as I was bigger than everyone else. At the last moment I thrust my frame forward with all the energy I could muster, just sufficiently to catch the closing doors. The impact flung them open again immediately. While everyone else paused to find the blockage I seized my opportunity and drove on through the startled and somewhat disgruntled clients of London Transport.

As the doors closed behind me I spotted Amanda. 'What took you so long?' she enquired.

We had to wait for nearly an hour at Euston Station with nothing to do. Neither of us felt like another game of Ludo. It was a very long hour. There was nobody else in our compartment on the way back to Birmingham for which I was very grateful. Darkness descended and Amanda went to sleep.

I sat by the window and looked into the glass. There reflected before me with the clarity of a mountain stream in bright sunlight was the mirror image of a discouraged failure who wanted to burst into tears but didn't know how. Somebody else was there too.

'I'm still here Peter,' God appeared to say, 'and I still love you.' If anything this seemed to make it worse. I didn't want love. I didn't want forgiveness. I wanted to return to Victoria Station and have another go.

'I can still heal her and bring her to myself,' I heard God say to the man in the window.

'I know Lord,' I eventually replied, 'and I pray that you will. I'm just so sorry. How could I? After all I've preached, and written, and desired for so long?'

God knew I didn't want an answer. I understood the theory only too well. Meet him at the cross. Find security, identity and worth only in Jesus. Seek first the kingdom of God. Ask him to come. Expect to see signs of his kingdom. Don't blame others if it doesn't seem to work. Be prepared for mistakes but don't let them stop the need to press on.

I suppose that was it. Just another case of falling short. God's love came on me and I too fell asleep. It seemed to be but a few moments before an excited voice startled me out of the security of my slumber.

'We're there,' exclaimed Amanda. Another time, another place, another chance to start again. The fount of Jesus' blood never runs dry. Carol's embrace and the hugs of my other children felt very warm. It's good to be loved when we make a blunder.

Endnotes

1. Dorchester is 'Casterbridge', Weymouth becomes 'Budmouth' and Sherborne is 'Sherton Abbas'. T.E. Lawrence may be better known to some as 'Lawrence of Arabia'.
2. It is my perception that demons do not foretell the future but through domination, manipulation and control try to make it happen. Their 'predictions' are simply boasts about what they are going to do. Once they have a few successes under their belts the victim receiving the messages comes more under their deceptive powers either through greater fear or the lust for power. We have, on occasion, been able to stop demonic prophecies from being fulfilled by casting out demons or breaking curses. But I am not surprised that a family spirit should correctly forecast what is going to happen to another member of the family. (A family spirit is normally considered to be one which tries to stay in a particular family. If it loses its home through death or deliverance it will normally try to enter a near relative. This is often what causes the feeling of deja-vu. There is frequently a group of them allowing demonic, or so-called telepathic or psychic communication to take place between one demonised member of a family and another.)
3. Leanne Payne, *The Healing Presence* (Kingsway Publications: Eastbourne, 1989), chapter two.